Transformations of Myth Through Time

JOSEPH CAMPBELL

Transformations of Myth Through Time

PERENNIAL LIBRARY

HARPER & ROW, PUBLISHERS, New York
Grand Rapids, Philadelphia, St. Louis, San Francisco
London, Singapore, Sydney, Tokyo, Toronto

Photograph credits appear on page 261.

The television series *Transformations of Myth Through Time* was produced by Dr. Stuart Brown and William Free, both of California. Dr. Brown is a physician/psychiatrist who practiced medicine for thirty years as a professor and clinician and is now writing and producing films. William Free is an independent film producer currently developing documentary and drama projects for television.

FIRST EDITION

Designed by Karen Savary

Photo research by Sabra Moore

Library of Congress Cataloging-in-Publication Data

Campbell, Joseph, 1904–1987
    Transformations of myth through time / Joseph Campbell. — 1st ed. Perennial Library ed.
        p.   cm.
    ISBN 0-06-055189-5 — ISBN 0-06-096463-4 (pbk.)
    1. Mythology.   I. Title.
    BL311.C278   1990
    291.1'3—dc20   89-45788

90 91 92 93 94   DT/MPC   10 9 8 7 6 5 4 3 2 1
90 91 92 93 94   DT/MPC   10 9 8 7 6 5 4 3 2 1 (pbk.)

CONTENTS

1

In the Beginning:
Origins of Man and Myth

The material of myth is the material of our life, the material of our body, and the material of our environment, and a living, vital mythology deals with these in terms that are appropriate to the nature of knowledge of the time.

This woman with her baby is the basic image of mythology. The first experience of anybody is the mother's body. And what Le Debleu called *participation mystique,* mystic participation between the mother and child and the child and the mother, is the final happy land. The earth and the whole universe, as our mother, carries this experience into the larger sphere of adult experience. When one can feel oneself in relation to the universe in the same complete and natural way as that of the child with the mother, one is in complete harmony and tune with the universe. Getting into harmony and tune with the universe and staying there is the principal function of mythology. When societies develop out of the earlier primeval condition, the problem is to keep the individual in this *participation mystique* with the society. Now, looking around, you see how little chance we have, particularly if you live in a large city.

Also we have the problem of the woman and the man in relation to mythological experience. In spite of what the unisex movement states, the differences are radical from the very beginning to the end. This is not a culturally conditioned situation. It is true also of animals, among Jane Goodall's chimpanzee friends, for example. One of the problems in human development is the long infancy. The child, until fifteen or so, is in a situation of dependency on the parents. This attitude of dependency, the attitude of

submission to authority, expecting approval, fearing discipline, is the prime condition of the psyche. It is drilled in. Also, the particular mores, the particular notions of good and evil and roles to play of the society, are imprinted.

One is born, is a blank—a little biological creature living spontaneously out of its nature. But immediately after it is born, the society begins putting its imprinting upon it—the mother body and the whole attitude of the mother. You can have a gentle, loving mother or you can have one who is resentful of the birth, which conditions a whole psychological, out-of-adjustment, situation. I was surprised to hear from Jane Goodall that the young chimpanzee also has a long period of dependency on the mother. And one of the psychological problems of the chimp is

the same as that which the human being faces, namely, after weaning and disengagement, to become actively, psychologically, disengaged from the mother.

Until very, very recently, the condition of the female in the human society has been that of service to the coming and maintenance of life, of human life. That was her whole function—the woman in the role of center and continuator of nature. The man, however, has a very short and ultimately unimportant relationship to this whole problem. He has another set of concerns. Jane Goodall's males control an area of some thirty miles circumference, and they know where the bananas are. When the bananas are failing in one area, they know where to go for more. They also are de-

fenders. They defend against invasions by other little tribes. And just in the primary way, the function of the male in this society is to prepare and maintain a field within which the female can bring forth the future. These are two quite different roles. And their bodies are made for them as well. The male is not engaged, like the female, in the constant charge of children. He has a lot of free time. He knows where the bananas are, but it isn't time to go there now, and nobody's bothering us, so what do we do? This is it; in men's clubs, delousing each other. So, this is a long-standing institution, the men's hunting team, the sports team, the men's club.

These are Hill Tribes people of New Guinea. Now the interesting thing about this is that this is a ceremonial battle, but serious. There is plenty of food. There is no need for one tribe to invade another to get their property. What are the men going to do? They are sitting around, with nothing to do, so they invent a war. This a war game, and the spears are serious. So, when one man is killed, the battle ends and then we have a period of waiting for another attack. This gives the men something to do. All the time they are on guard against the other one launching the return attack, preparing for it. The male has to have something serious to do, that's all.

The male body is built for combat, for defense. It is a fact that, in the human body, every muscle has an impulse to action and one is not fully alive unless one is in action. So we have the invention, always, in societies of games. Games of strength, games of cleverness, games of winning, as in ancient Greece. In the male community what is important is the ranking, the pecking order, what Jane Goodall called "Alpha Male"—who is Alpha Male? Who is top male? In a charging display, a fellow comes down the line pulling down branches, and anyone who wants to claim top male position has to challenge him in this action. The winner is top male. She describes one little fellow, who was anything but a top male, who found that by kicking oil cans around he could

make quite an impression. For a couple of days, before everyone else caught on, he was top male.

Jane Goodall described a very interesting episode which struck me, and I bring it forward as a little suggestion. She was seated on a hill slope, observing through glasses a number of her chimpanzee friends over on the opposite slope of the valley. There were half a dozen males, and females of about the same number, and a few of the little ones. It was pouring rain, and suddenly there was a prodigious thunderclap and the males went bananas. They started charging displays one after another. When I heard that I recalled that the philosopher Giambattista Vico (1668–1744) had suggested that the first notion of the godhead arose out of experiencing the voice of the thunder. The voice in the thunder is the first suggestion of a power greater than that of the human system.

The male chimpanzee is almost twice as heavy as the female. There is no question about physical supremacy. This applies largely to the male/female in the human sphere as well. Here is Theseus abducting Antiope, the queen of the Amazons—the power of the male and the female submission to it. The female is physically vulnerable. Also, she is booty, and one of the problems of the male is to protect the females of the community from abduc-

tion. This is a long-standing situation, and the breeding of the race favors these two opposed physical organizations. And so the myths have to deal with this, and the male body and the female body have their symbolic values throughout the system.

Now, as for biological spontaneity, a young female chimp takes her younger brother or sister as a doll and imitates mother and plays with the child. Males don't do this. The young male starts pushing young females around. Then he starts pushing older females around. When he gets to be really big and strong he enters the men's group and finds his place in the pecking series. Two entirely different spontaneities. Two very different natures.

It used to be thought that the thing that distinguished man from the beast was his toolmaking. *Homo habilis*, man the toolmaker. Yet a female chimp made a little sheaf of reeds. She pulled the leaves off and prepared a system of tools for herself. She poked the reed down a termite hole, and the termites down there grabbed it, and then she drew it out and licked them off. After she did this for a half hour or so, the reed began to get soft. So she threw it away, picked up the next one she had prepared, and went on. It went on for two or three hours this way, like some woman eating candy and reading a French novel. But she actually had tools here.

Now we come to an artist's representation of an australopithecine. This is one of the, well, perhaps the earliest grade of hominid that has yet been identified. This is in south and east Africa. This type of creature is now being pushed back to something like four or five million years ago. He has picked up a tool and is running, but the important thing is the legs. Apparently the first essential development of the hominid, distinguishing him from the arboreal ape, is this kind of running leg, which released the hands. The way in which apes walk uses the knuckles of the front legs or arms. It used to be thought that the brain enlargement was the main distinction; not so anymore. It was the legs. This left the hands free for manipulation, and then the brain increased.

A hand from southern Ethiopia from four-and-a-half million years ago shows no knuckle walking. This is a human hand already, four-and-a-half million years ago. Now this first type of human being, when we get above the australopithecine, which has the brain capacity simply of an ape, is the

Homo habilis, as he is now called, with a brain capacity a little larger than that of a male gorilla, something like 800 or so cubic centimeters. Beyond that, then, we come to the second grade of man, known now as *Homo erectus,* an early example of which was *Pithecanthropus* from Java, called Java man. The brain capacity here is up around 900 cubic centimeters.

We also have tools from this date, about 500,000 B.C.—practical tools. If apes could handle stone and break it, the tools would be practical tools of this kind. But there is a particular tool that, for me, represents the emergence of a human type of consciousness— the birth, you might say, of the spiritual life such as no animal would ever have invented. This tool, also from 500,000 B.C., was found on the banks of the River Thames. It's larger than what would be useful, about six inches or eight inches long. What Robinson Jeffers, the California poet, calls "divinely superfluous beauty" is here.

There are two types of human beings. There is the animal human being who is practical and there is the human human being who is susceptible to the allure of beauty which is divinely superfluous. This is the distinction. This is the first little germ of a spiritual concern and need, of which the animals know nothing. Since this

tool is larger than what would be practical, the suggestion is that it must have been used in some sort of ritual context. So there is a slight suggestion here of the probability—the possibility, if not the probability—of some sort of ritual action, probably associated with the meat or food that is to be eaten.

We come now to *Homo sapiens*. This is the first order of *Homo sapiens, Homo sapiens neanderthalensis*, Neanderthal man. He used to be the one that was called the ape man, but we find that his brain capacity in some cases is over 1,600 cubic centimeters, and the brain capacity average today is less than 1,600 cubic centimeters. So we've got to pay our respect to this chap. He was a tremendously powerful figure that emerged and took the land just south of the great glaciers of the Riss-Würm glaciation, the last glaciation, appearing somewhere around 200,000 B.C. and surviving until about 40,000 B.C. That's a long, long season. And I want to stress him. This is *Homo sapiens*. The brain has come to a certain size and there is a transformation of consciousness and it's at this period that the first infallible signs of mythological thinking appear. And they appear in two aspects.

The first is of burials. In a burial from about 60,000 B.C., from Mount Carmel, in what is now Israel, the jaw-

bone of a boar was found. In other words, a sacrificial offering has been associated with the burial. The body is in the crouch position of the fetus—returned to the womb. This is the first experience of mystery beyond that of the magic of divine and superfluous beauty. This character was our friend: walking around, warm, talking. He lies down, something departs, he's cold, stiff, and begins then to decay. What has left him? The notion that what has left is still alive is what we experience here. Burial with grave gear. It is in this period of Neanderthal man that the first burials appear. Some remarkable burials have recently been found in northern Iran and Iraq of Neanderthal man from about 60,000 B.C. At Shanidar, a male, a powerful male, was buried with flowers on top. The pollens remain and have been identified, most of them of medicinal plants. He may have been a shaman of some kind. But beyond that, beneath him were the bones of two women and a child. Do we have a suttee burial here already? We don't know. The date is about 60,000 B.C. So, the human spirit lives on beyond the wall of time that we know, and one relates to it.

One of Jane Goodall's apes' tiny little babies died of polio. A polio plague struck the little community. This poor female had no idea what had happened, and she just walked around for days holding the little thing in her hand until it began to stink. Then she took it over her shoulder, walked off into the forest, and came back without it. Something has happened, but there is no conscious relationship to it; there is no way to handle it, to turn it into something significant. That is the opposite to the human experience system.

Now we go back to Neanderthal times. There were two signs of the beginning of mythological experience and thinking. First was human burial, the second is worship of cave bear skulls. In the high alps of Switzerland and Silesia there have been found half a dozen small cave chapels in which there are cave bear skull caches, hiding

places where cave bear skulls have been kept. Some of them have rings of stone around them. Others have the long bone of the bear in the bear's mouth, as though the bear were eating its own flesh. Others have the long bones poked through the eyes—fear of the evil eye, apparently. But just as the human being who has died is still there, so is the animal who has been killed still there, and we have to take care of revenge, malice, and so forth.

Now the typical system of belief among hunting people who are killing and eating animals all the time and do not feel, as we do, that the animal is a lower form of life, is that the animal is an equivalent form in another aspect and is revered, is respected and yet killed. The basic mythic theme of

hunting cultures is that the animal is a willing sacrifice. It comes willingly to be killed. You can find this in the myths all over the place. But the animal comes with the understanding that it will be killed with gratitude, that a ceremonial will be conducted to return its life to the mother source for rebirth, so that it will come again next year. There is also the idea of a specific animal—that is, you might say, the Alpha Animal—to whom the prayers and worship are addressed that are to concern the entire animal community. It is as though there were a covenant between the animal and the human communities honoring the mystery of nature, which is: life lives by killing. No other way. And it is the one life, in two manifestations, that is living this way, by killing and eating itself. And so perhaps already, in this figure of the cave bear skull consuming its own flesh, we have that image of what life is, which I think is the prime image.

Today we don't kill the animals we eat. We have butchers who do that, and the food comes all nicely packed, particularly in the shopping centers. You see people throwing this one around, or that one, saying, "Oh, I'll take this." It's a different attitude. These people thanked the animal for having given itself. We thank our notion of divinity for having given us this meal. It's a totally different psychol-

ogy, a totally different mythology. The prime one is this of life, in its various manifestations, consuming itself.

In northern Japan, in Hokkaido, there remains a race of people that is Caucasoid, not Mongoloid. They are known as the Ainu and their principal cult is a bear cult. This is *today*, forty thousand to sixty thousand years later. The conservatism of primitive man is basic. To change a form, even of a tool, is to lose its power. And so you have here a cult from 60,000 B.C. still in northern Japan among the Ainu people. There is a sanctuary of black bear skulls of the Ainu, the counterpart of the caves in Switzerland from sixty thousand years ago. Now this idea, the animal master, is basic: the covenant of the animals, the notion of the physical as being secondary to the spiritual life's energy, a ritual of thanks and of returning the energy to its source for another visit.

Now we come to later *Homo sapiens*, Cro-Magnon man. This order of the human species appears around 30,000 to 40,000 B.C. and appears not only in Europe, where he was first discovered, but also in Southeast Asia and in two or three other places, as though there was a parallel evolution taking place. This reconstruction by W. K. Gregory is based on the first Cro-Magnon skull that was found in the Dordogne. Known as the "Old Man of

Cro-Magnon," this is the man who did those beautiful works of art in those great caves.

Among the first images were Paleolithic Venus figurines, as they are called. They stand a few inches high, and now something like two hundred of these have been found in a belt stretching from the Atlantic coast of France and Spain right across Asia to Lake Baykal on the borders of China. They are all of essentially the same type. There is no action on the face at all, no face whatsoever, and there is great emphasis on the breasts and hips and loins. Here is the miracle of the female body, the mystery of the female body, which gives birth to life and

nourishment to life—that mother we were talking about in the beginning. There are no feet, and this is explained simply by knowing that they were made to stand up in little household altar shrines. Two or three have been found actually *in situ*. These little figures are associated with dwelling sites, rock shelves under which the community lived. They do not appear in the big caves, only in dwelling sites. This is the mother of life. She is symbolic of that which all women incarnate.

This figure is from a shelf in France called Laussel, and it is a very important and suggestive figure. This little Venus of Laussel is holding in her right hand, elevated, a bison horn

with thirteen vertical strokes. That is the number of nights between the first crescent and the full moon. The other hand is on the belly. What is suggested—we don't have any words of writing from this period—is a recognition of the equivalence of the menstrual and the lunar cycles. This would be the first inkling we have of a recognition of counterparts between the celestial and earthly rhythms of life.

Alexander Marshack, in his formidable volume *The Roots of Civilization*, deals with a number of staves, or staffs, of this kind which are notched. He studied a number of them with a microscope and found that the notches were not made by the same instrument at the same time on any one piece. He says these are probably time-factored counts. Many of them suggest very strongly counts of the lunar cycle. So maybe, out of the women's concern for this rhythm that they will have recognized in their own bodies, we come to mathematical and even astronomical reckoning.

This figure is known as the Venus of Lespugue. It has been damaged and so it isn't so beautiful as it once must have been. But I'm presenting this to demonstrate that these are not naturalistic; they are aesthetic compositions. Brancusi might have been interested in this. The whole magic of the woman is brought here into one circle. The breasts and the hips brought down together, and then you have that elegant sweep of the chest to the head and then the feet, where she was made to stand in a little shrine. These figures date from around 18,000 B.C., the Magdalenian times, or even earlier.

Turning to the problem of the male in this society, we go into the great temple caves. Nobody would live in these caves. They're cold, they're dangerous, they're dark, and they are frightening. The general consensus of scholarship is that they represent the sanctuaries of the men's rites, where boys were turned into men. And what they had to learn was courage. They had to undergo death and resurrection rituals. They died to their dependent infancy, and they came to maturity as self-responsible, active, protecting males. And they had to learn also not only the art of the hunt but also the rituals of the hunt.

This particular figure is known as the Sorcerer of Trois Frères. An enormous cave, something like a mile in its reaches, in the Pyrenees, it is called Les Trois Frères because three brothers, playing with their dog, discovered it. The dog fell down a hole, and when they went down that hole they came into this fantastic cave. The main chamber is an enormous chamber with this figure dominant. The chamber is now entered through artificial openings, but originally, apparently, it could be entered only through a long flume, like a pipe, about fifty to seventy-five yards long, through which one had to crawl, as though it were a rebirth theme. One of the great scholars in this field, Herbert Kühn, has described crawling through it, and if you're susceptible at all to claustrophobia you would hardly get through. Well, one can imagine a team of four or five youngsters being sent through, and when they came out the other end, this is what was looking at them. And all around the rest of the cave are engravings of animals: the animals of the great hunting plains. The hunting plains were abundant in animals, like the animals of the Serengeti. The Sorcerer is part human, part animal. This is the animal master in a ritual context. The evidence for shamanic action in these periods is very convincing. He has a lion body, and the placement of the genitalia in the rear is of the feline. The legs are of a man, the eyes are possibly of an owl, or of a lion, the antlers of the stag. The stag loses his antlers annually, but he brings them back again and so is an incarnation of the forest spirit. Any animal that has an annual cycle, for instance, the peacock

losing his tailfeathers, becomes symbolic of the process that moves the seasons. So this is the mysterious Sorcerer of Les Trois Frères. Does he represent a deity, or does he represent a shaman? There's been an argument on this, but it doesn't make any difference whatsoever. Because the shaman, in that form, would be the deity.

We keep thinking of deity as a kind of fact, somewhere; God as a fact. God is simply our own notion of something that is symbolic of transcendence and mystery. The mystery is what's impor-

tant, and that could be incarnate in a man or in an animal; or not incarnate but recognized in a man or in an animal. George Catlin, in the northern Missouri River among the Mandan Indians, painted a Mandan shaman, an animal man. In one of the caves of France, there is the same dancing figure.

In the great cave of Lascaux, in the Dordogne, in what is called the rotunda, another great chamber, there is a frieze of animals. On the left corner is this strange beast with these strange

horns. No animal in the world looks like that, and yet these artists painted animals in a way that no one's been able to paint them since. So what did they have in mind here? We will go to Australia. It is remarkable the continuity from these caves to Australia and what we can find. Here is an Australian elder in a ritual costume with the same "pointing sticks," as they are called there. Now the pointing stick has been described at length by Géza Róheim in his study of Australian psychology. The pointing stick is a negative phallus; instead of generating, it kills. With certain whispered magical charms it is pointed between the legs at the enemy, and the enemy will then

be killed by being ripped open from the rectum to the genitals.

At Lascaux, in the crypt, a lower chamber, this famous image appears. This definitely is a shaman. He's got the masked head of a bird on his *baton de commandement*. Here is the erect phallus, the negative phallus, the pointing stick; and by miracle a lance has struck through the animal master here, which is a bison, and opened up his guts exactly as the pointing stick would have worked. This particular figure has brought about a great deal of discussion. Some writers have suggested it represents a hunting accident, which is ridiculous. What we know about magic would indicate that if a hunting accident were depicted in the most sacred place of a sacred cave, it would produce hunting accidents by sympathetic magic. What it certainly represents is the bison. The principal animal of the hunt is the principal animal master. The bison is invoked in the name of the covenant, animals giving their lives willingly through the power of the shaman.

The whole idea of the men's sacred ground, the men's cave, is continued in ceremonial huts which are associated with rebirth. You enter the tiny little door as though it were the vulva and go into the mother body and everything inside is magical. We're in a magical field. When you go into a cathedral today, you are in a magical field. And the men who are in there are not this individual, that individual, another individual, they are in a role. They are the experiences of the energy of nature coming through them.

In a great cathedral such as Notre Dame de Chartres, our mother church, the mother body, you're in the magic realm again. The imagery is that of dream. The imagery is that of myth. The imagery is that of reference to transcendence. On the west portal of Chartres is a mandala actually symbolic of the vulva and the womb, and the second coming, the birth. And just as the great prime magician was portrayed in the caves, Pope Innocent III is portrayed here. Now there are two ways of coming into this role, one is temporarily for the ceremony, another is permanently. Here is a Maori chieftain, permanently in the role. His whole body is tattooed. He's got a

magical body. That is to say, the stained-glass windows and incense and all have been imprinted on him. He's in the cathedral all the time, you might say. His life is that of a mythological role.

So much for the first crisis—that of maturation from infancy to maturity. We come to the second, marriage, where one becomes one member of a two-fold being. This beautiful thing from Athens is a fifth-century, red-figured ceramic piece, and it shows a woman initiating a man. Actually, in a marriage, woman is the initiator. She is the one closer to nature and what it's all about. He's just coming in for illumination. This becomes especially interesting because this is Thetis and Peleus, the mother and father of Achilles. So it is a marriage. Thetis was a beautiful nymph with whom Zeus fell in love. Then Zeus learned that her son would be greater than his father and so Zeus thought better of the relationship and withdrew and saw to it that she should marry a human husband. So Peleus is her human husband and she is a goddess. And the text tells us that when he went to take her in marriage she transformed herself into a serpent, into a lion, into fire, into water, but he conquered her. Well, that's not what you see here at all. She has power that is symbolized in serpent and in lion.

Let me repeat the basic story of the sense of these two symbols. The serpent sheds its skin to be born again as the moon sheds its shadow to be born again. The serpent, therefore, like the moon, is a symbol of lunar consciousness. That is to say, life and consciousness, life energy and consciousness, incorporated in a temporal body—consciousness and life engaged in the field of time, of birth and death. The lion is associated with the sun. It is the solar animal. The sun does not carry a shadow in itself; the sun is permanently disengaged from the field of time and birth and death, and so it is absolute life. These two are the same energy, one disengaged, the other engaged. And the goddess is the mother personification of both energies.

One serpent is biting the youth between the eyes, opening the eye of inner vision, which sees past the display of the field of time and space. A second serpent is biting under the ear, opening the ear to the song of the music of the spheres, the music, the voice of the universe. The third serpent is biting the heel, the bite of the Achilles tendon, the bite of death. One dies to one's little ego and becomes a vehicle of the knowledge of the transcendent—becoming transparent to transcendence. That was the sense of the initiations that we have been reading about. The woman becomes a ve-

hicle at the time of her menstruation, and the man in his ceremonial is a vehicle as well.

And so to the world of art. The two hands—this is important—good and evil together. The yin-yang cycle. Chinese. The mystical dimension is beyond good and evil. The ethical dimension is in the field of good and evil. One of the problems in our religion lies in the fact that it accents, right from the very start, the good and evil problem. Christ comes to atone for our sins, evil atonement. The first people to listen to St. Paul were the merchants of Corinth, and so we have the vocabulary of debt and payment in our interpretation of the mythic themes. Whereas in the Orient, the interpretation is in terms of ignorance and illumination, not debt and payment. The debt and payment explanation goes haywire when you realize there was no Garden of Eden, there was no fall of man, and so there was no offense to God. So what is all this about paying a debt? You have to read the symbols in another vocabulary now. Furthermore, we have to deal with the assumption and ascension to heaven. What heaven? Going at the speed of light, the bodies would not be out of the galaxy yet. Your mythology, your imagery, has to keep up with what you know of the universe, because what it has to do is put you in accord with the universe as known, not as it was known in 2000 B.C. in the Near East.

This beautiful work is from a wall in

Pompeii. This young man is being initiated. There is an initiator and an assistant. The boy is told, "Look in this bowl, it is a metal bowl, and you will see your own face, your own true face." The bowl is of such concavity inside that what he is going to see is not his own face at all but the face of old age held behind him. And isn't that a shock! He is being introduced to what our American Indians call the "long body," the whole body of your life from birth to death. And so, again, we have the mythology of the long body. Now suppose one of his friends, before he went in there, said, "Now look, you see, this guy, he is going to have a bowl there and he is going to tell you you're going to see your own face. You're not. He's got another fellow there and he's holding this face of an old man." There would be no initiation. There would be no shock. That's why mysteries have to be secret; because what is experienced is experienced for the first time.

23

2

Where People Lived Legends: American Indian Myths

This picture is from W. B. Yeats's curious and remarkable book *A Vision*. Yeats took it from an alchemical work of the sixteenth century, *Speculum Hominum et Angelorum (The Mirror of Men and Angels)*. What it represents is the cycle of the moon as a counter-

part to the cycle of a human lifetime, with the fifteenth night of the moon corresponding to the thirty-fifth year of a lifetime. Using the terms that Yeats applies to this, we are born from the transcendent mystery and immediately the society begins putting its imprinting upon us. The mask that we are to wear is put on us by the society. Yeats refers to this as the primary mask.

The eighth night of the moon is the night of adolescence, of puberty. At that time, light begins to dominate over darkness, and so the attitude of dependency and submission has to be transformed now into one of maturity. There are two kinds of maturity, however. There is that of a traditional society, where the individual moves over into the role of the authority which has been that of the society. Let's say he becomes the executor, the one who administers the rituals that carry the sense of the culture. He continues in the way of the primary mask. On the other hand, in our culture world we have a more open view. The individual at this time may be able to have the sense of a destiny and a world work of his own of which the society has no notion. We begin to get a separating.

The individual begins to find his own path and the drag, you might say, of the primary mask is gradually thrown off. This is what is known as the left-hand path. The right-hand path is that of living in the context of the ideology and mask system—persona system—of one's local village compound. The left-hand path is that of the individual quest. Each of us is an individual. Earlier societies did not pay much attention to this. In our world, particularly in the European world, the individual is recognized as a positive, not simply a negative, power. And so there comes, in our world, the antithetical mask—the mask of the individual's own life, pulling against the other.

Even where the youth is encouraged to find his own path, there is nevertheless a psychological lag, so this is a period of great tension. We are not reborn as easily as primitives, or as people in traditional societies. We have a more complicated birth. We come then to the fifteenth night of the moon. Now the image here is of these two great lights: the lunar light, which dies and is resurrected, and the solar light, which is independent of the vicissitudes of time. At this moment, the moon and the sun are equivalent lights. Out on the plains on the fifteenth night of the moon, at the time of sunset, looking to the west, you see the sun at a moment just resting right on the horizon. And if you look there to the east, the moon will be in the same position on the eastern horizon. I have seen it twice in my lifetime and both times mistook the moon for the sun.

This is a moment of great mystical importance. Here your consciousness, your body and its consciousness, are at their prime. And you are in a position to ask yourself, Who or what am I? Am I the consciousness or am I the vehicle of consciousness? Am I this body which is the vehicle of light, solar light, or am I the light?

I once had the task of talking about these matters, talking about Buddhism, in fact, to a group of prep school boys, youngsters between the ages of about twelve and seventeen, and when it came to this problem of explaining what this Buddha-consciousness or Christ-consciousness was, I looked up at the ceiling for an inspiration and I found one. I said, "Look up, boys, at the ceiling and you will see that the lights (plural) are on, or you might also say the light (singular) is on, and this is two ways of saying the same thing." In one case, you are placing emphasis on the individual bulbs, in the other you are placing emphasis on the light.

Now, in Japan, these two alternatives are called, respectively, the *Ge Hokkai* and the *Ri Hokkai*: *Ge Hokkai*, the individual realm; *Ri Hokkai*, the general. And then they say *Ge, Ri, Mu Gai*: individual, general, no obstruction. Same thing. Now when one of those light bulbs breaks, the superintendent doesn't come in and say, "Well, that was my particularly favorite bulb." He takes it out, throws it away, and puts another one in. What is important is not the vehicle, but the light.

Now, looking down at all your heads, I ask myself, of what are these the vehicles? They are the vehicles of consciousness. How much consciousness are they radiating, and which are you? Are you the vehicle, or are you the consciousness?

When you identify with the consciousness, then, with gratitude to the vehicle, you can let it go. O Death, where is thy sting? You have identified yourself with that which is really everlasting. This consciousness that throws up forms and takes them back again, throws up forms and takes them back again. And then you can realize that you are one with the consciousness in all beings. You are one with them and you can say *Ge, Ge, Mu Gai*: individual, individuals, no obstruction. This is the ultimate mystic experience on earth.

That's the crisis here. The death and resurrection of the eighth night is death to the infantile ego, birth to the mature. Here is death to the body, identification with the eternal aspect of this in the body, and from then on it's a wonderful thing to watch the body go, following the course of nature. Until the twenty-second night of the moon, darkness begins to preponderate; the body becomes more and more submissive to the primary rules of the society and of nature. I remember one gentleman asked, when I was talking about this, "When does it happen?" I said, "You'll find out soon enough."

Then we have, in the center, these signs indicating the nuclear moment of the crisis. *Temptatio*, temptation, the cup of Tristan and Isolde. Not of Isolde and King Mark, the marriage arranged for by the society, but the awakening of the meeting of the eyes and the awakening of the individual destiny and its realization. Then here is pulchritude, beauty, the glorious moment. Then we come to the decline and violence against yourself, holding yourself in form for the last lap. And finally, *sapientia*, the fruit, wisdom. Not a bad score.

And so this also is part of the mythology of the body, the body going through its inevitable course—the long body. In a beautiful painting by a Swiss artist of the nineteenth century, Bolkin, Death is playing the violin to the artist. That is the serpent bite on the Achilles tendon which opens the two eyes. He is no longer just himself, he is the vehicle of the voice of the muse.

The following for me epitomizes the sense of the early man in his relationship to nature. This famous speech was given by Chief Seattle, after whom the city of Seattle is named, around 1855.

The President in Washington sends word that he wishes to buy our land. But how can you buy or sell the sky, the land? The idea is strange to us. If we do not own the presence of the air and the sparkle of the water, how can you buy them? Every part of this earth is sacred to my people. Every shining pine needle. Every sandy shore. Every mist in the dark woods. Every meadow. Every humming insect. All are holy in the memory and experience of my people. We know the sap that courses through the trees as we know the blood that courses through our veins. We are a part of the earth and it is part of us. Perfumed flowers are our sisters. The bear, the deer, the great eagle, these are our brothers. The rocky crests, the juices in the meadow, the body heat of the pony, and man, all belong to the same family. The shining water that moves in the streams and rivers is not just water but the blood of our ancestors. If we sell you our land you must remember that it is sacred. Each ghostly reflection in the clear water of the lakes tells of events and memories in the life of my people. The waters' murmur is the voice of my father's father. The rivers are our brothers. They quench our thirst. They carry our canoes and feed our children. So you must give to the rivers the kindness you would give any brother. If we sell you our land, remember that the air is precious to us. That the air shares its spirit with all the life that it supports. The wind that gave our grandfather his first breath also receives his last sigh. The wind also gives our children the spirit of life. So if we sell you our land, you must keep it apart and sacred as a place where man can go to taste the wind that is sweetened by the meadow flowers. Will you teach your children what we have taught our children, that the earth is our mother? What befalls the earth befalls all the sons of the earth. This we know. The earth does not belong to man. Man belongs to the earth. All things are connected like the blood that unites us all. Man did not weave the web of life, he is merely a strand in it. Whatever he does to the web he does to himself. One thing we know, our God is also your God. The earth is precious to Him. And to harm the earth is to heap contempt on its creator. Your destiny is a mystery to us. What will happen when the buffalo are all slaughtered? The wild horses tamed? What will happen when the secret corners of the forest are heavy with the scent of many men and the view of the ripe hills is blotted by talking wires? Where will the thicket be? Gone. Where will the eagle be? Gone. And what is it to say goodbye to the swift pony and the hunt, the end of living and the beginning of survival? When the last red man has vanished with his wilderness and his memory is only the shadow of a cloud moving across the prairie, will these shores and forests still be here? Will there be any of the spirit of my people left? We love this earth as a newborn loves its mother's heartbeat. So, if we sell you our land, love it as we have loved it. Care for it as we have cared for it. Hold in your mind the memory of the land as it is when you receive it. Preserve the land for all children, and love it as God loves us all. As we are part of the land, you too are part of the land. This earth is precious to us, it is also precious to you. One thing we know, there is only one God. No man, be he red man or white, can be apart. We are brothers, after all.

Compare that with Genesis 3. And you see what's happened. Furthermore, the land is the holy land. And the land where you are, not the land someplace else. Not only the body, but the specific landscape in which the people are dwelling is sanctified in these old mythologies. You don't have to go someplace else to find the holy place.

And that's the theme that I want to develop. I'm going to take, as the model for this sanctification of the land, the world that we're in here, the world of the Navaho and the mythology of the Navaho and their sand paintings. I want to run through a series of these sand paintings and the mythic matter associated with them. The people of Iceland have a term, *land-nam*, which means "land-claiming" or "land-taking." Land-taking consists in sanctifying the land by recognizing, in the features of the local landscape, mythological images. Every detail of the Navaho desert land has been sanctified and recognized as a vehicle of the radiant mystery.

In this sand painting what you get are the four directions, the colors as-

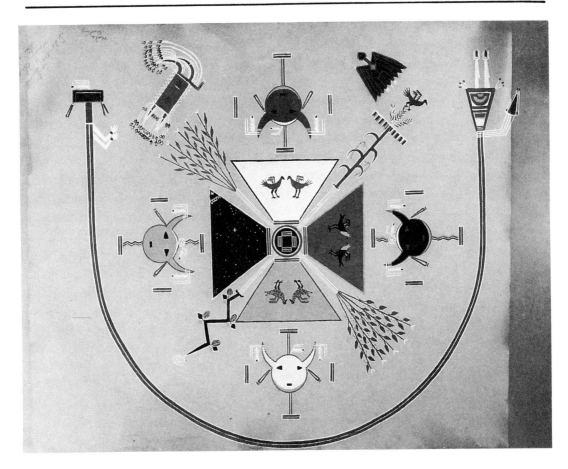

sociated with each of the four directions, and the center. The center is dark, the abysmal dark out of which all things come and back to which they go. And when appearances emerge, they break into pairs of opposites. This is all basic mythological stuff that we find in India. The sun rises in the east. It is the place of birth, of emergence, new life. When the Buddha achieved illumination he was facing east. The New Testament is a testament of sunday, the rising of the new eastern sun. In the height of the sky, the blue sky of noon, is the midpoint, the thirty-fifth year of life. In the west the sun sinks, and in the north the sun is underground. The north is always an area of awe and mystery and danger, the danger of that which has not been accommodated in the forms of the social order. So we see the sun in these various aspects.

Now all of these mandalas are open to the east, not closed, open, to receive the transpersonal, the transcendent light shining through. All things are to be transparent to transcendence. When a deity like Yahweh in the Old Testament says, "I'm final," he is no longer transparent to transcendence. He is not, as the deities of the older cultures, a personification of an energy which antecedes his personification. He says, "I'm it." And when the deity closes himself like that, we too are closed like that, so we're not open to transcendence either. And you have a religion of worship; whereas when the deity opens, you have a religion of identification with the divine. And that was what Christ mentioned when he said, "I and the father are one," and he was crucified for it. Halaj said the same thing, and all of these are saying the same thing. We are particles of that mystery, that timeless, endless, everlasting mystery which pours forth from the abyss into the forms of the world.

Just as the animal of the hunter, the animal that is the principal animal of his life, becomes the animal master, so when planting comes in, the main plants are sanctified also. There are Pueblo myths and Huichol myths in Mexico, telling of the corn maidens. One of them, in one of these myths, is compelled by the young hero's mother to grind the corn, and as she is grinding, her own arms disappear. And she disappears. She is grinding herself away. Our whole life is sustained by the mystery life, and everything that you eat, whether vegetable or animal, is a life that is being given to you through its own willingness to become your own life substance.

So all of these mandalas are placed with the east at the top, and it's open. And then there are the guardians of the gate; in this case they are a little figure known as Donso, Big Fly. I'm told that as one walks on the desert sometimes a big fly comes down and sits on one's shoulder. This big fly is the counterpart of the Holy Spirit. It is the voice of the mystery and it is your guide. And it can be called "Big Fly" or in another aspect "Little Wind." And isn't this interesting? It is the wind, *spiritus*, the spirit, we got in Chief Seattle. That's an archetype, the recognition of breath as the breath of life.

Just as the plants are sacred, so is the buffalo. This is the buffalo mandala and the surrounding horizon is of mirage. There are two buffalo guardians at the gate and people of the myth

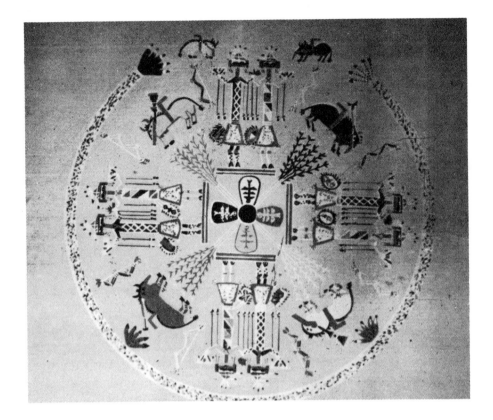

stand in the four directions, the central source with Donso figures. And there are also the main plants. These are the corn maidens of the four directions, the corn and the maiden. They appear either as corn or as maiden. Again, in the center, the dark with the crossing of the rainbow, the rainbow miracle.

Now I want to go back to the main myth of the Navaho. It's a Pueblo myth as well. It's the one that is universal in this part of the world. It is of the first people having come up from the womb of the earth through a series of four stages, and they go from one stage to another. Some accident happens in the lower stages; a flood comes as a punishment for impropriety of some sort, the breaking of a taboo or something of the sort, and they come on up. And finally they come to the top level, the earth on which we are now. This is really an out-of-the-earth birth. There is a ladder of emergence and the first people are with the plants and the animals roundabout that they discover here, and there is a special kind of mirage enclosing it.

At the Museum of Modern Art in New York, some years ago, a team of

Navaho singers came to show sand paintings and how they were made, and it was marvelous to watch these men take colored sand in their hands and with great precision prepare these marvelous paintings. When they would prepare them, they would always leave out one detail. Now, when they were given to artists, such as these have been given to artists, to copy and then store in that Museum of the Navaho Art, something will be left out. That is to protect those who are dealing with the painting from its power. They are not supposed to have the power turned on. Well, they made one painting in the museum and then they were asked, "Couldn't you just complete one painting, complete this one for instance?" and they laughed and they said, "If we finish this one, tomorrow morning every woman in Manhattan would be pregnant." So, these things carry power. It was also interesting to watch them when the paintings were being destroyed, when they were being removed. They took that sand, and the only thing I could think of was a Roman Catholic priest with the consecrated host in his hand. There was sacred power here. They were not just brushed off and thrown away, they were put in a special container and taken somewhere else of which we know nothing.

So here's the first part of the legend, the legend of emergence. Now I said that in Iceland we have this concept of *land-nam,* land-claiming. A specific place is identified on the reservation as the place of emergence. It wasn't the place of emergence; it is the ritual symbol of the place of emergence. And you consider the emergence mystery when you address yourself to that place. There's the mountain of the north and the mountain of the south and the mountain of the east and the mountain of the west. The land is consecrated. It is a holy land in this way. Where did the myth come from? It came with the people to that place. And then they consecrated the place in terms of the myth that was with them.

Now I want to go through a specific legend—the legend of "Where the Two Came to Their Father." These paintings are not sand paintings but pollen paintings. They are made of ground-up corn and ground-up petals, flowers, and so forth. When the Second World War started and the young men on the Navaho Reservation were being drafted into the army, there was an old singer there named Jeff King. A friend of mine, Maude Oaks, went down to the Navaho country to learn the legend lore and to make paintings. Well, she had, really, to seduce the old men into giving their stories to her and the thing that persuaded them was the realization that the young men weren't learning these things anymore. These rituals are of one night, three nights, or nine nights. And the singer has to know by heart an extremely elaborate mythology and ritual system. And there must be no mistakes and there is always a second singer to supervise to make sure that no mistakes are made in the chanting.

Young men are not putting themselves to learn all this anymore. And so, the rituals are dying out. The plea was that if they would give to the modern anthropologist investigator this material, it would be stored and would be kept as a treasure in the museum of the Navaho. At that time, this is back in the thirties, the normal Navaho family is described as having been of a father, a mother, one child, and two anthropologists. The Navaho was a real hunting ground for the anthropologist. Well, when a young man would be drafted, his family might go to old Jeff King, who had been a military scout for the American army when they were fighting Geronimo and the Apache. King died in his middle or late nineties and is buried as a military hero in the cemetery at Arlington. Well, Maude got him to give her the rite that he was performing over the young men going into the army. It was an old warrior ritual called "Where the Two Came to Their Father."

Having emerged from the underworld, the people were settled in this little place here, and in the four directions are the mountains of the four directions filled with the seeds of all things. This is the house of Changing Woman, a wonderful figure in the Navaho mythology. She was born, miraculously, of a cloud, and she became the mother then of two boys by miracle, by virgin birth. She was bathing at a little spring and the sun shone upon her, and when she came home she gave birth to a little boy. There were monsters troubling the neighborhood and so she dug a little hole and put the boy down there in a kind of underearth cradle to protect him from the monsters and then went back to the spring to wash herself, and she conceived again, this time of the moon. And so she comes back and here are her two little boys. The boy who was born of the sun is called Killer of Enemies. He is the warrior, outward directed. The boy who was born of the moon is called Child of the Water, and he is the medicine man, the shaman. The twin hero motif is common to many, many mythologies of the world. They represent the warrior chieftain and his magician priest.

Well, they are living with their

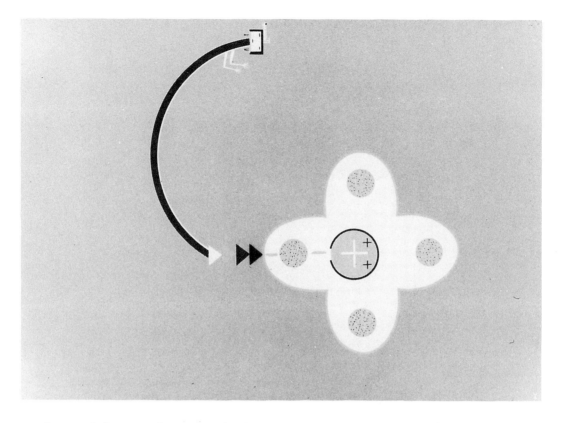

mother and they see that not only their mother but the whole neighborhood is being troubled by monsters and so they think they had better go and get help from their father, the sun. (The sun is ultimately the father of them both, because the sun lights the light of the moon.) Now, their mother had told them, "It's dangerous around here, boys, and you can go to the east, to the south, to the west, but don't go north." So they go north. That's the only way to get new material. Don't obey the community. They're the ones that are stuck or in trouble. So, guided by Rainbow Man, they go to the mountains, the four corners; everything in the American Indian mythos is in fours. They circumambulate the world and are on their way. Now this is a typical hero quest myth.

When they come to the end of the known world, that's to say, when they reach the horizon, they are confronted by this threshold guardian whose name is White Sands Boy. He is the guardian at the east. He has long arms. He seizes people and buries their head in the sand and so smothers them. He is the one who sees to it that

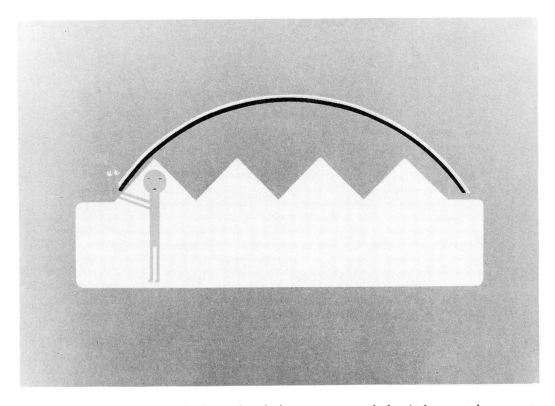

people don't go beyond the bounds of the mythology. The boys give him praise. They say, "O wonderful White Sands Boy, there never was a thing in the world like you." And he'd never received such praise in his life, and so he said, "O.K., you can go on." And they make the rounds, there's White Sands Boy, and Blue Sands Boy, and so forth, and now they are beyond the bounds of the world.

They're going along in a kind of featureless landscape and they see an old, old woman and her name is Old Age. And she says, "Well, hello, boys, what are you doing way out here, you earth people?" They say, "We are on our way to our father's house, the sun, to get weapons to save our mother from the monsters." "Oh," she says, "that's a long, long way. You'll be old when you get there. But I'll give you some advice. Don't walk on my path. Walk to the right of it." So the boys start walking along to the right, but then they forget. Heroes always forget. And they are walking on the path again and they begin to feel old and they have to pick up sticks and walk with these and then finally they can't walk at all and Old Age, the old woman, has been watching them and she comes in, "Ah, ah, ah, I told you." They say, "Can't you make us young

again?" "Well," she says, "if you'll be careful now, I'll do that," and so she spits on her hands and takes moisture from under her armpits and from between her legs and she rubs it over them and they're made young again. And she says, "Now you stay on the right of the path."

So they go along and pretty soon they see another little old lady, a black little old lady. This is Spider Woman. Now these spiders lived in the ground and this is kind of a fairy godmother, the counterpart of the fairy godmother. She is the spirit of the earth mother itself in the form of the old spider. "Oh, hello, earth boys, what brings you out here?" "Oh, we're on our way to our father, the sun, to get weapons to save our mother." "Oh, that's a long, long trip. You'd better come down into my little house and I'll fix you up for that journey."

And so she made the sun go fast (she has power over the sun itself), so that it should set and they'd have to spend the whole night with her. They thought it was a very little hole. How can we fit through that? But when it came time there was no problem at all. They go down and she feeds them certain food and gives them certain pieces of ebony and turquoise to swallow and fixes them up for the journey and tells them what the problems are going to be, that they're going to meet, and she gives them a feather to protect them. "Hold this feather close and you will

get through all obstacles," the cactus that cuts, the reeds that pierce, the rocks that clash together, and so on.

Well, with these to help, the boys start on their path and they do pass through the obstacles. Standard stuff. We've gone past the known world. Magical help comes to us in the form of some fairy godmother. Ways of the journey are predicted and overcome. The boys then come to the ocean that surrounds the world. That's a standard mythological motif. The *Okeanos* of the Greeks. We know that it surrounds the world because here are the four mountains of the four directions.

In other words, they have translated space into a flat picture. In these pictures, the animals are not rendered naturalistically. These people know how to render all these things naturalistically. They're rendered in the form of their spiritual reference. The transformation of nature in art is rendering the nature phenomenon transparent to transcendence.

The boys, with the feather between them, now cross the water by the magic power that has been given them. They approach the house of the sun, which is guarded by four types of animal guardian. First we have the four serpents. The young man who is being trained to be a warrior, having his psychology transformed from that of secular to military consciousness, comes walking in along this line, kneels down here with his head over this basket of yucca suds. He undergoes a ceremonial washing, a purification; you have purification before you have the revelation, and that's the sense of this rite. There are also guardian bears, guardian thunderbirds, and guardian winds. The boys, having passed these, come to the house of the sun. It's a microcosm of the macrocosm, with the four directions. Here is the sun's daughter, here is the sun's horse. He rides around the world with his sun shield. These are the steps of the boys, and pauses where they meet the obstacles on the way.

They arrive. The sun is off on his daily trip and the boys are met by the sun's daughter. She says, "Who are you?" They say, "We are the sons of the sun." "Oh you are, are you? Huh! Well, uh, Daddy's not home now, but when he comes home he's going to make it tough for you, so I'll protect you." And she wraps them in clouds of the four colors and stores them over the doors of their proper color. Over

one door she stows Killer of Enemies and over the other Child of the Water. So in the evening the sun arrives, gets off his horse, comes into the house. He hangs his shield on the wall and goes clunk, clunk, clunk, clunk, clunk, clunk. Then he turns to his daughter and says, "Who are those two young men I saw coming in here today?"

She says, "You always told me you behave yourself when you go around the world. These boys say they're your sons."

"Oh they do, do they?" So he searches the house, and he pulls them down and then he submits them to tests.

This is a favorite motif in American Indian stories. The father test, or the father-in-law test, or whatnot. He throws them against spikes of the four colors in the four directions. Flint spikes. They hang onto the feather. They survive. He gives them poison tobacco to smoke. They survive. He puts them in a sweat lodge and tries to sweat them to death. They survive. He finally says, "Well, I guess you are my sons. Come into the next room." So he takes them into the next room. He stands one of the boys on a black buffalo skin, the other on a white, and he tells them their true names and each acquires his own true character. You remember before they were both black and the same size. Now they're taller

and Child of the Water is blue. Well, the description of that moment of initiation in that room, where the thunders come in and lightnings come in, is something terrific, but now they know who they are. This is the second birth through the father, the same thing we've been talking about.

When they have survived, they are so powerful they split into four. The yellow is the counterpart of Killer of Enemies and the white the counterpart of Child of the Water. And, now in full power, they start back across the cosmic ocean. They come to the hole in the sky. Now, the feather that they're riding on here is not the one that Spider Woman gave them. It's one their father has given them. Their father, now at the hole in the sky, gives them a final examination. "What's your name? What's the name of the northern mountain? What's the name of the hole in the earth?" The answers are whispered to them by Big Fly and Little Wind. Now you might say this is cheating, but it isn't cheating. If they weren't worthy of this, they would not have received the inspiration. So, there you are; if you are meant to pass the exam, you'll pass. So, having passed the exam, they come down to the central mountain, Mount Taylor.

Now, before they go to work to kill the specific monsters that were trou-

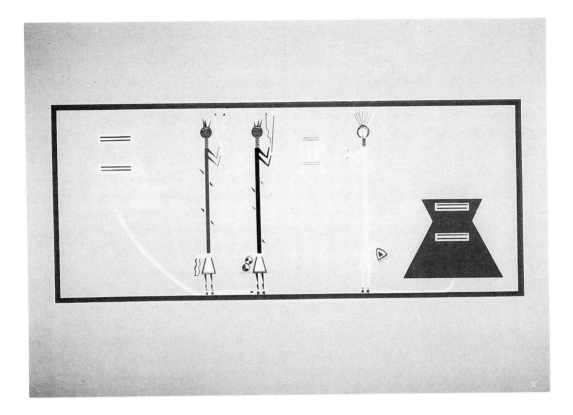

bling their mother, they have to kill the archetypal monster, and he lives by this lake. His name is Big Lonesome Monster. Now, the characteristic of monsters is that they mistake shadow for substance, and so this Big Lonesome Monster sees the two boys reflected in the lake. "Oh, yes. I can drink them up and digest them to death." So, Big Lonesome Monster, mistaking shadow for substance, drinks up the lake and digests hard and then spits it out again, and there they are. He drinks up the lake four times. Now, even a monster's worn out after that performance. And so the boys move in. Now, interestingly, this monster is also a son of the sun. But the sun moves in to help the boys kill the monster—ambiguity about virtue and vice and pairs of opposites and all that.

So the monster is killed and now they are ready to go home. When they come past the foot of Mount Taylor, they trip and lose their father's weapons. They have moved from the realm of sheer male fire into the mixed realm of water, where the fire is mingled with earth. And so they are met by Talking God, who is the male ancestor of the female line of the gods. He is mixed of male and female and he gives them a talking prayer stick made of male and female corn to guide them. They are given double weapons—male and female weapons. And this energy coming from them in the form of flints indicates that they are filled with magic power and they are still riding on the feather. Talking God's mouth and eyes are made of masculine rain and female mist coming up, in this form. His nose is of a corn stalk. He has given them the weapons to kill the earthly monsters. After a terrific series of battles, killing these tremen-

dous monsters, the boys are nearly wiped out. They're so worn out they've lost their arms and legs and Child of the Water is in danger of just becoming the reflection of Killer of Enemies. And so the gods come down and enact a ceremony over them, and they're given health again. And what do you suppose the ceremony is? It's the one I've just told, the ceremony of their own life story—just as the psychoanalyst leads you back to remember all those things of childhood and to put you on your proper path again. When they have passed this test and

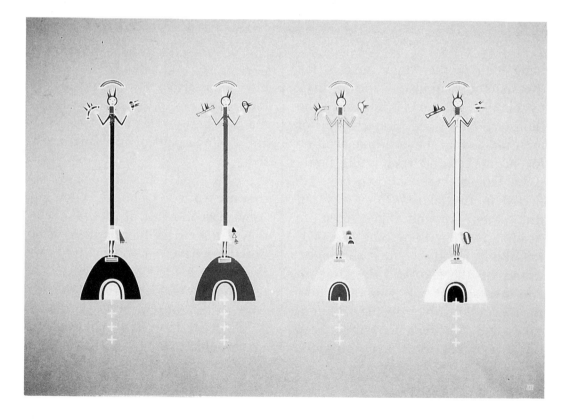

BLACK ELK AT THE CENTER OF THE EARTH

gone through this ceremony, they are, again, four. This is the strongest sand painting of the lot—the four boys, each standing on the mountain of his own color.

When Maude Oaks received this ceremony from Jeff King, he omitted this picture. He said, "Well, that's it." Maude said, "No, Jeff, there must be another picture." Now she knew enough to know what was required in those mythological ceremonial situations. "No," he said, "I've given you everything." "No, Jeff," she said. "O.K.," he said, "I'll give it to you."

So we've got the whole story here. This is typical mythological adventure. Leaving the bounded world in which you have been brought up, going beyond all that anybody knows into domains of transcendence, and then acquiring what is missing and coming back with the booty—a perfectly beautiful example of this system.

This painting was made by a friend of Black Elk. John Neihardt's book *Black Elk Speaks* is a beautiful book. Fortunately it was a poet who received this message from old Black Elk, who was in his nineties, of the vision that this guardian of the Oglala's medicine pipe had experienced when he was a boy of nine. The vision foretold, in a magical way really, the destiny before his people. It came to him long before they had had their first encounters with the cavalry and the Battle of Wounded Knee. Old Black Elk, when he was quite a youngster, fourteen or so, participated in the battle against Custer. At one point in his vision, he said, "I saw myself on the sacred, central mountain of the world." Here he is on the central mountain of the world with the axial tree, and the three birds around about, and Matthew, Mark, Luke, and John roundabout as well. He said the central mountain of the world, the highest mountain, is Harney Peak in South Dakota. And immediately after that, he said, "But the central mountain is everywhere." Now there's a man that knew the difference between the folk cultic symbol and the reference of the symbol.

The holy land is everywhere. And so when you come into a landscape for the purpose of the cult, and worship so that you can address your minds to the mystery, designate this is the center, this is the north, this is the south mountain, and so forth. This word of this wise old man reminds me of a sentence, comes from a text of the twelfth century that was translated from Greek into Latin called the *Book of the Twenty-Four Philosophers*. It says there, "God is an intelligible sphere"—intelligible means known to the mind—"an intelligible sphere whose center is everywhere and circumference nowhere." And so it's right here. The function of the ritual and the myth is to let you experience it here, not somewhere else a long time ago.

I would say that there's no conflict between mysticism, the mystical dimension and its realization, and science. But there is a difference between the science of 2000 B.C. and the science of A.D. 2000. And we're in trouble on it because we have a sacred text that was composed somewhere else by another people a long time ago and has nothing to do with the experience of our lives. And so there's a fundamental disengagement. When we look back at that text, it is a text that speaks of man as superior to nature, man's mastery over nature as being what has been given to him. Compare that with the words of Chief Seattle. This is the difference between mythology as a petrifact, something that has dried up, is dead, and is not working, and mythology as something that is working. When the mythology is alive, you don't have to tell anybody what it means. It's like looking at a picture that's really talking to you. It gets to you. If you have to ask the artist, "What does that mean?" if he wants to insult you, he'll tell you. The myth must work, like a picture. It can be explicated if you've already experienced it, interpreted and amplified, and so forth; but it must work. And we've lost it.

An article from *Foreign Affairs* called the "Care and Repair of Public Myths" says that a society that does not have a myth to support and give it coherence goes into dissolution. That's what's happening to us. He defines myth in an incomplete way. He defines it as an order of acceptable ideas concerning the cosmos and its parts and nations and other human groups. But it concerns also the mystic dimension that informs all this. If that's not there, you don't have a mythology, you have an ideology. It concerns also the pedagogy of the individual, giving him a guiding track to guide him along. And that's what the myth that I've just given you does. It coordinates the living person with the cycle of his own life, with the environment in which he's living, and with the society which itself has already been integrated in the environment.

3

And We Washed Our Weapons in the Sea: Gods and Goddesses of the Neolithic Period

The next great stage is the emergence of the city civilizations—the beginning of historic processes. A remarkable thing happens, in certain places, at certain times. The timeless idyll of the nature religions yields to a temporally ordered process. Civilizations emerge that have histories: a youth, a maturity, and an aging. The most important representation of this in literature is in Oswald Spengler's *Der Untergang des Abendlandes—The Decline of the West*. He discusses eight civilizations that have gone through these cycles and indicates exactly where we are.

There are three main centers that have been recognized as matrices of origin of agriculture and the domestication of animals. They are southeast Asia, which is now recognized as

49

probably the earliest center; the area that comprises southwest Asia, Asia Minor, and southeast Europe; and, of course, Middle America, Mexico, and Peru.

In the Near East, high culture cities, writing, and high mathematics developed. Here, the principal agriculture is of grains. The animals domesticated are cattle, and then later the horse and in the Syro-Arabian desert area the dromedary, the camel.

We start in south Turkey, in Anatolia, in a little town called Catal Huyuk. There's a very important series of excavations here, conducted by James Mellaart, which lowered the antiquity of planting cultures in the Near East down to about 10,000 B.C. Catal Huyuk is situated on a plain, and the village is a little bit like the pueblos of the American Southwest. Houses are packed one on the other. To take such a town by storm you have to tear the

buildings down. There is no way to get into the town except by way of the buildings themselves. There are some fifteen levels of these buildings at Catal Huyuk. This is one of the most important and oldest finds, and it is the key symbol of the main mythology of this area. Here you have the mother goddess back-to-back with herself. On the left she is embracing an adult male, and on the right she holds a child. She is the transformer. Where you have agriculture as the base, the goddess is going to be the primary mythological figure, personifying the energies of nature which transform past into future, transforming semen into child, seed into produce.

This small piece, made of a green schist, dates from 7000 B.C. It was found in a grain bin, and so it is associated with agriculture. It's a ceramic of the goddess seated between two felines. You remember our association of the lion with the goddess? She has given birth, and we can see the head of a child. From Rome, about A.D. 100, we have a figure of the Anatolian goddess, flanked by lions, seated on a throne, with the sun disk in her hand and on her head the crown, the Walled City. Here the city has arisen. During the Carthaginian wars, the cult of this Anatolian goddess was brought into Rome as one of the supporting powers to support the Roman cause. So here we have seven thousand years of this goddess.

A great number of little chapels have been found at Catal Huyuk, and in one of them, associated with the goddess, we have a figure of two facing leopards. These are the threshold guardians, the male and female leopard defending the sanctuary. The spots on the leopard are trefoil, three-leaf forms.

Here is a drawing of a typical little

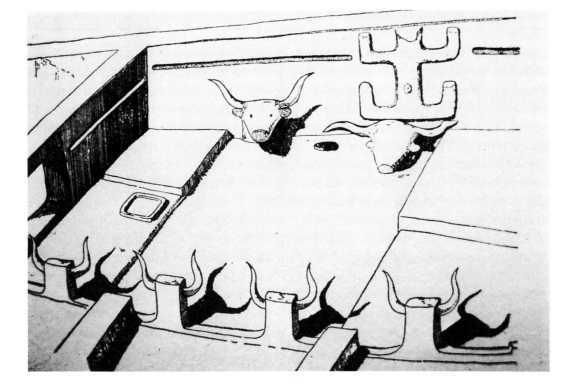

shrine room, with a form of the goddess called, by the excavators, the birth-giving form. And what she has given birth to here is not a human child, but a bull. Now, we have no writing from the period, but the bull, later, is associated with the moon. The moon dies and is resurrected and is born again from the solar goddess. In the grain bin figure, we have her giving birth to a human form and here to the symbolic bucranium, the head of the bull.

In another fascinating chapel is a mural with the bull's head, the returning moon, with a skull under it. We have already spoken about the skull cult. On the wall is a vulture eating a body that is without a head. The head or skull has been removed. The body is returned to mother earth, or mother sky. The vulture is the consuming aspect of the goddess who gives birth; the body is therefore being recycled, as we would say today. If you were to translate into words the sense of this little shrine with the skull, it would be, "O Goddess Mother, as the moon is reborn, so may I, my mortal body being returned to the source."

The excavations in Jericho were conducted under the supervision of Kathleen Kenyon, just about the time that Mellaart, working in Catal Huyuk, uncovered on a wall (ca. 6000–5000 B.C.) another of these vulture murals, where the goddess is consuming bodies from which the heads, which apparently contain the consciousness, have been removed. Representations of this vulture goddess—her name is Nekbet—cover the whole ceiling of the tomb of Ramses VI in Egypt. So this cult lasted six or seven thousand years.

In southeast Europe, in the past thirty years or so, a tremendous amount of material has been excavated. There is a magnificent study of these materials by Marija Gimbutas, from the University of California at Los Angeles. Her book is called *Goddesses and Gods of Old Europe, 7000–3500 B.C.* This is very early, and it's a period when the mother goddess is dominant. I want to review a series of im-

ages associated with northern Greece principally, but also the Balkans and the areas around the Danube, Dnieper, Dniester, and even a little bit of the Volga. In a 6000 B.C. representation of the goddess, there are a number of traits that are essential. One is the towering neck; this is the world axis. She is the axis. There is a bird figure on the top of the neck. She is bird goddess and spiritual goddess, but also obviously a human female with breasts. Associated with her is the boar. The labyrinth is another recurring theme incised on ceramic serpents, jars, and statues.

On the inside of this bowl, which dates from 5000 B.C., is what looks like a linear script. If it is, this is the earliest writing in the history of civilization. The date usually given for the origins of writing is about 3200 B.C. in Mesopotamia, in ancient Sumer.

There is a male figure of a ruler from

this period, and over his shoulder is a scepter in the shape of a reaping sickle. An actual sickle of copper from that date, 5000 B.C., survives, so these are agricultural people harvesting a grain of some kind. Their tools are not weapons. They are heavy copper tools and they are used for carpentry and/or agriculture. These are peaceful cities. It's only later that walls begin appearing that indicate raids coming in from outside. We're approaching, with these walls, the whole history, later history, of the Near East.

First we have planting people in high mountain valleys and later in the great river valleys: Tigris, Euphrates, and Nile. Then there are the barbarians raiding in from the desert and the great plains. There are two orders of barbarians: the Semites, from the Syro-Arabian desert from the south; and the Indo-Europeans, from the north. The Indo-Europeans were herders of cattle. It is they who first domesticated the horse and invented the war chariot, which became an invincible weapon. The Semites were herders of sheep and goats, and they first domesticated the camel.

The gods are of two orders really: those that represent the powers of nature, which operate in the universe and within ourselves; and those that are the specific patrons of the tribe. In most mythologies, the tribal patron deities are secondary to the nature deities. In Semitic mythologies, the role is reversed. Around 4500 B.C. the early minotaur appears—a human head and the bull's body. Sometimes it is reversed—a human body and a bull's head. So we have the minotaur, the bull and cattle as a principal deity—just as the bison was among the American Indians. The animal and human forms become mixed, just as they were in the early dancer at Les Trois Frères.

Around 3500 to 3000 or 2500 B.C., in Crete, we find a continuation into the island world of the mother goddess system that had flourished on the mainland. Meanwhile, on the mainland, patriarchal warrior people, herders, are raiding in and the culture is changing. You have a marginal survival in Crete of the earlier mother goddess systems. She is depicted with the laboris, or double axe, which is the prime symbol of Crete. She not only is the one who gives life, she is the one who takes it. There are lunar suggestions in the crescent form of the blades —death and resurrection. In Crete the prime animal is the bull with the horns. The moon must die to be resurrected. The sacred bull is slain and the young bull is the resurrection.

The bull sacrifice seems to be a substitute for an earlier king sacrifice.

Here we see bull games depicted in a little mural in the palace at Knossos in the king's chamber. There's been a question as to whether bull games of this kind, of people leaping over bulls, are possible. It's a shorter-legged bull than the *toro bravo* of the Spanish bullring, and yet it still seems an impossible feat. Well, when I was a student in France I went down to Bordeaux to see a bullfight. There the bull isn't killed. There came into the bullring a collection of chaps in white duck pants and white shirts with red sashes. Trumpets of triumph greeted them. Most of them were lame from having met the bull in one encounter or another; and after they had saluted the congregation, a young bull with horns like needles was released into the arena. The thing was to get this bull to run at you and then to step aside, moving only one foot. So you can imagine that there were some moments of horror. This was going on very nicely when one of the chaps, when the bull came at him, ran at the bull and jumped right over the bull. Years later, I thought, Did I dream this? No, I did not. The practice lives on in France. So, it can be done.

The floor plan of the palace of Knossos is a kind of labyrinth. The question is, Where did the bull games occur?

People used to suggest it was inside the palace, but that would be too dangerous. There's a big slope outside and probably they were held there. Young women as well as young men participated. In one mural women are dancing, much like the girls that dance at halftime of a football game. And the whole audience is women. In none of the archaic cultures are women as elegantly prominent as in Crete. There must have been some kind of continuation there of the women's role in the earlier mother goddess culture systems.

At Knossos there's a tiny little throne room. On the king's throne there is carved the moon that dies to be resurrected. The Cretan king was killed possibly once every eight years

in association with the cycle of the planet Venus. You don't see pictures of old kings in Crete. On either side of the throne we have a griffin.

Where you have women prominent in a cult there is most likely going to be an accent on what might be called the religious experience rather than on the theological, logical, and rational aspects. It's much more the experience accent. In a depiction of a dance, the female figures have the heads of griffins. So the griffin is somehow associated with the goddess cult.

Here is a tomb ceremony, with the dead person, the tomb, and offerings. The moon boat carries the soul to the underworld and there are animal sacrifices. The giant altar horns at Knossos, through which you see Mount Ida, the sacred mountain, were put there by Sir Arthur Evans, but he

knew what he was doing. Here is the goddess on the cosmic mountain with her lions, the feline animal, and behind her the altar horns and the trident, the way between the pair of opposites—the way to transcendence.

It is in the Near East that the first cities appear, and here is something entirely new. The culture life of a small community or nomadic tribe would be pretty well available to everybody in the community. You would have a community of equivalent adults. The distinctions would be age group distinctions, male and female distinctions, and the distinctions between the normal order of people and especially gifted, shamanic visionaries. But with the enlargement of the communities that followed the establishment of agriculture and the domestication of animals, we begin to have a differentiation of professions. Instead of a culture of what might be called generalists and amateurs, we have professionals, people whose whole life and the whole dynasty of their family is devoted to government or the priesthood or trade or agriculture. So we have a differentiation of peoples and a new problem, namely, to get people of different life forms to experience themselves as members of a single organism. And that's what is disintegrating in our world. With the worker against the employer, and this against that, and so forth and so on, there is a disintegration of the cultural organism.

In the early cultures the problem was to keep the organization intact. With the professional priesthood, there was a recognition of the passages of the planets through the zodiac of the fixed constellations. These were the people who invented writing, arithmetic, and numeration in terms of sixties and of tens—the sexagesimal and the reckoning by tens. We still use the sexagesimal for reckoning cycles of time or of space. With writing, mathematics, and precise observation of the heavens, it was possible to determine that the planets were moving at a mathematically determinable rate. So we begin to get an idea of a cosmic order that could be mathematically recorded. This is a whole transformation of culture, and something altogether new and different comes in. In the earlier situations this peculiar tree, this special pond or rock, the exceptional becomes important. Later it is the ani-

mal that is of most importance, or the plant. But now we begin to have the notion of a cosmic order, and the exception is out rather than in. The exception is aberrant. And so we have a totally new way of regarding the universe.

In the Tigris-Euphrates area, the earliest cities in the world first appear. The entry into these river valleys occurs somewhere around 4000 B.C. About the same time there's also an entrance into the Nile valley. The Nile is a kind of oasis area protected on all sides by desert. The Tigris-Euphrates is something quite different. They're wide open—north, south, east, and west—to invasions. And so, whereas something very stable evolved in Egypt, there were enormous transformations and historical developments in the Tigris-Euphrates area.

Among the early finds that we're going to be dealing with are those from Halaf, very early pottery, 4000 B.C., and from Samarra. Uruk and Al-Ubaid were very early cities. This is a beautiful example of Halaf from about

4000 B.C. Now, it's in this period, and in precisely this kind of work, that the notion of an aesthetic field first appears. When we go to the caves, you don't have an aesthetic field. You have a great organization of forms in terms of the structure of the cave, but you don't have an enclosed area like this. Also, the designs here are more abstract. So abstraction and an aesthetically organized field begin to appear. The pottery here, which is very early pottery, is extremely fine. It's an elegant ceramic period. For example, the bucranium, the bull's head, is arranged in such a way as to make a Maltese cross. Aesthetic composition and arrangement have become significant. In Samarra, we find a whole constellation of swastika forms and animals going around in a counterclockwise fashion. The swastika represents the four points of the compass, the cross of the earth in movement. There is another piece of ceramic ware with women and scorpions in a circular pattern—the circumambulation motif, circumambulating the cosmic tree. We're going to see this theme again in a surprising context—two animals, a kind of reversed mirror image, sharing a single set of legs.

One of the earliest little temples that has ever been excavated and reconstructed is at Al-Ubaid and comes from around 3500 B.C. The huge temple compound is in the form of the vagina of a cow. You have the cow goddess, the universe as cow mother. The milk of the cow is the milk of the goddess. In the compound was a herd of sacred cattle, cared for by the priests. The sacred milk of the sacred cattle would be fed to the ruling house. It is holy food. These are the same sacred animals that are walking the streets of Calcutta today. There's a continuity here of the cow, the mother universe. The four feet of the cow are the four points of the compass. The same imagery appears in Egypt.

Now we come to the lion form. Here is the lion pouncing on the cow, or on the bull in this case. The sun pounces on the moon; the lion pounces on the bull. An equivalent symbol is the eagle pouncing on the serpent. The moon sheds its shadow; the serpent sheds its skin. The eagle is the solar bird; the lion is the solar animal. This figure dates from 3200 B.C., from Sumer, the earliest high civilization in the world. It is an enormously important and impressive figure. This is the bull. The

sacred beard indicates a ceremonial and symbolic animal with the bull's horns. He's being consumed by the lion eagle. This lion bird is a Sumerian representation of the solar power constantly consuming the bull. Life comes, life goes. One foot is on a crescent form here on the top of the cosmic mountain. The cosmic mountain is the earth goddess. Here is the generating power of the bull. It is reminiscent of those flints that appeared in the Navaho, representing energy and power. This is the same kind of motif from the joints of the bull.

This serpent madonna is from Babylon. When this was first discovered in the 1920s, it was thought perhaps to be a foreview of the fall in the Garden of Eden in the biblical tradition, because the Book of Genesis, the mythology in the Book of Genesis, is largely an adaptation of Sumero-Babylonian myths. But there's a very different spirit here. This is the cosmic tree, the axial tree. Here is the goddess of the tree, and here is the serpent who sheds its skin to be born again. The association of goddess, serpent, and tree recalls the Garden of Eden, Eve, and the serpent. And here comes the male moon figure for refreshment. He comes here to receive the fruit of eternal life for refreshment. This is not a fall. There's no idea of a fall in these traditions. In India, the deity enters the world voluntarily, as a dance. The world is a play; it's a game. That's the mood you have in these mythologies. It's joyous, humorous at least. There's no more dreary mythology in the world than that of the Old Testament.

The Warka vase, from Uruk, is from the same period. Unfortunately, the vase is broken so we don't see the king, but we do see his train and the servant carrying it. A priest brings offerings to the priestess of the temple. Within the temple are offerings that have been brought. The Sumerian priests bringing the offerings go before the shrine naked. We go before God naked. The flocks, the sheep and goats and so forth, which are to be increased through these offerings, are also represented.

You remember the little Paleolithic figure of the woman as muse, as inspirer of the spiritual life? This figure here is the first thing of this delicacy and sweetness that we have in the history of sculpture. The eyes originally would have been of blue lapis lazuli, and there would have been a wig on the figure. When we think now of mother cults, everybody talks about fertility. But that's not the main inspiration of the goddess. That's only on the physical level. This is woman as muse. On the spiritual level she's the mother of our spiritual birth as well, the virgin birth, the birth of our spiritual life; and that's certainly what's represented here. This is one of the most beautiful things from this whole period. Other representations of the goddess and god in this aspect lack the delicacy of this work, but they tell us something of the accent. These are called eye goddesses. The accent here is in the spiritual realm; the blue eyes are the eyes of the heavens. There is a male deity in this tradition, and in one work we can see the blue eyes, and the face is quite specifically a Semitic face. So the Semites are coming in from the desert. People of the Akkad and the Moabites, these ones and those ones, the Ammorites and so forth, pouring in and becoming assimilated. Indeed, there is an eye goddess shrine with just the eyes.

Now we come to 2350 B.C. and Sargon I. This is the first known important Semitic emperor in this zone. These people have come in from the Syro-Arabian desert, first as conquerors, then as rulers. This beautiful bronze is from 2350 B.C. Sargon was born of a humble mother in the upper

reaches of the Tigris. She put him in a little basket of rushes, which had been made watertight by pitch, and confided him to the waters of the river. He floated down the river and was pulled out of the river by a gardener on the royal estate. The goddess loved him and so he advanced in rank and presently became ruler himself. This is, of course, just about two thousand years earlier than the text with which we are familiar. Sargon is the first conqueror for whom we have praise and celebrations of victory.

About this time wars of conquest come into being. Formerly, wars were simply revenge wars or ceremonial wars like the ones in New Guinea. A village would be raided and that was it. But now we have substantial conquest with hymns and celebrations. There is wholesale tearing down and annihilating of cities. And a refrain comes back: "And we washed our weapons in the sea. And we washed our weapons in the sea." So, here it is, about 2400 B.C., the beginnings of the kind of war that has been distinctive of our world, of civilization, ever since—ruthless annihilation of whole populations. Read the Book of Judges, read the Book of Joshua. You get plenty of it.

There was an early Sumerian period in Ur, 3300 or 3500 B.C. or so, then a Semitic invasion with Sargon I, and then a Sumerian restoration, a resurgence, about 2000 B.C. Most of what we know about the mythology and architecture of ancient Sumer dates from this Ur number three and the Lagash periods, 2000 B.C.

At the ziggurat of Ur, the lower manifestation of the deity was shown to the people down below. But up on high, where heaven and earth are married, you have the esoteric cult of the priesthood. The same thing occurred in Middle and South America.

Sir Leonard Woolley, excavating at Ur, came upon the most amazing burials. Whole courts had been buried alive. There is a reconstruction at the University of Chicago Museum of one of the great royal tombs at Ur. Whether the king was killed or died a natural death, we do not know. He could, in fact, have been just a high priest king who became a sacrificial offering.

The bullock carts and drivers that brought the body in, the officers of the court, the girl dancers, and the musicians were all buried. The hands of the harpists, the skeleton hands, were at that place on the harp where the strings would have been had they not decayed.

There were two orders of women in the tomb. One wore gold headbands

67

and the other wore silver. One of those wearing silver was found not to have the headband on her skull, but it was all wrapped up and at her hip. She had been late for the party and had not had time to put her crown on.

Above this tomb of the king was the tomb of the queen. So it's a suttee burial in high style. Her court is also buried along with her. The figures lie in regular rows and many of them have a little cup at their side in which there had been probably henbane or something of the sort to put the person to sleep while they were buried.

Now this business of mass burial, whole courts buried, continued in the Near East into very late times. The history of the early dynasties of Egypt are filled with this. In China it was continued until the time of Confucius and Lao-tzu, both of whom mention it as something abominable that should not be continued.

The Banner of Ur is the representation of a military expedition and contains the earliest known pictures of chariots. The wheels did not revolve on the axles; the axle revolved with the wheel. So they were very clumsy chariots. The animals pulling them were not horses but asses. The brilliant horse-drawn war chariot comes much later. We see the victory feast of the *potaze*, the principal governor, with his

court, probably drinking beer or mead. These were not wine drinkers. The cattle are being brought in for the feast. There is also a figure standing with a harp, and on the harp's head we see the figure of the bull.

We have hymns from this period of the bull god, the moon god, Dumutse, who has gone into the underworld and sings for his goddess to come and bring them both to eternal life. The great heroic deed of the goddess is the descent, stage by stage, to the underworld to bring eternal life to both. This is the idea of suttee. The husband and wife are one. When he dies or is sacrificed, she must follow. And the two together are then brought to eternity through her heroic act.

From this time also we have about the earliest examples of animal fables. The animals play human parts. We have the simulation of a sacrificial offering; the simulation of a dance, with a bear doing the dancing; and a scorpion man in the abyss.

Now we come to about 1750 B.C. and this is Hammurabi of Babylon. It's from his period that the great epic of Gilgamesh comes. Hammurabi received the law from the god Shamash, the sun god. You see the sun rays from his shoulders. As Moses received the law from Yahweh, so Hammurabi from Shamash. Urnamu, the lord of

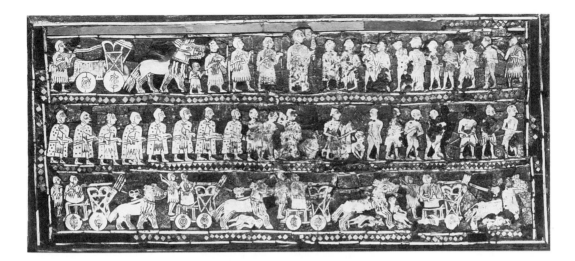

the great city of Ur, from which Abraham is supposed to have departed, also received the law from the sun god. And when the law comes with that kind of a backing, it can't be fooled around with. The law was, of course, invented by Hammurabi but attributed to God. And we can say the same for Moses.

pains me to speak of God in the third person."

I raised my hand and I said to Dr. Buber, "There's a word being used here today that I do not understand." He said, "What is that word?" I said, "God." "You don't know what God means?" I said, "I don't know what *you* mean by God. You're telling us God has hidden his face, nobody sees him today. I've just come from India, where people are experiencing the face of God all the time." So what does he say? "Do you mean to compare?" The moderator cut in and said, "No, doctor, Mr. Campbell just wants to know what you mean." So he said, "Well, we all have to come out of our exile in our own way." But the Indians aren't in exile. Because God is right in them.

These are the differences that have to be recognized when you're talking cross-culturally, about religions in terms of comparative religions. Compare? Yes, I do compare. It's my job. Those are different ideas.

So what we have in India is a tendency towards syncretism, accent on the universal deities, with tribal deities who are the local patrons but belong to the larger system. You don't have different systems in different places. You have one great system with local ancestral patrons.

Here we are in Mycenae about 1500 B.C. Before the invention of the horse collar, which rests on the horse's shoulders, and so the weight is pulled from the shoulders, the vehicles were drawn by a band across the horse's

chest. The horse's windpipe is out front, so that if you have a heavy vehicle, he chokes. They could not invent a really usable war chariot, a flexible one, until they had mastered a race of very powerful horses. As you see, very light chariots were used, and their invention took place around 1800 B.C. in those differentiated Indo-European plains culture spheres.

In the great Mycenaean Acropolis, one burial includes a chariot with the two horses that drew it. A Chinese burial of the same date also has two horses, the chariot, and the charioteer. Different race, same culture. A page from the Mahabharata shows the great chariot warriors of India, and we have representations of Tutankhamen in the same chariot, about 1340 B.C. You can see it's from the same tradition. This is what's known as diffusion from a creative center, a new idea goes out

and with it go the deities and energy symbols in association with it.

We move now to Egypt and the Nile. Egyptian history is quite easy to follow because the earliest period is in Lower Egypt, the middle period is in Middle Egypt, and the final period is in Upper Egypt. From around 4000 B.C., we have this figure of the goddess. This mural, from the period known as Badarian, is from the tomb at Hierankopolis. It is a tomb with two chambers, which suggests suttee again. There's nothing Egyptian about the mural. It looks much more like something from Iran. There are the interlocked animals such as we saw in Samarra, 4000 B.C. But this is about five hundred years later. So the influences are coming in from Mesopotamia and inspiring a development in Egypt. Here are the figures of dancing animals and figures going around the

center. All are motifs from Iran. And then suddenly around 3200 B.C., the First and Second Dynasties, we have the arrival and development of a specifically and indubitably Egyptian art form which remains for three thousand years. This is called the Narmer Palette. King Narmer of Upper Egypt, wearing the crown of Upper Egypt, is subduing the pharaoh, or whatever he was called, of the delta. Here is Narmer's totem animal, the hawk, with the king of the delta by the nose. Here is the papyrus swamp of the delta, and here are the enemy slain. We also have a cow figure, Hathor, the goddess of

the horizon. She appears in four aspects. The king is wearing a belt and a bull's tail. He is the moon bull incarnate. The pharaoh is the highest god. He is Osiris, the moon bull incarnate. And on his belt are the face forms of Hathor in front, in back, and on either side. The pharaoh fills the horizon. On the reverse side is Hathor again, and the king now wears the crown of Lower Egypt, of the delta. We see the symbols of his pharaonic power, the dead of the delta's armies, and the animals symbolic of Upper and Lower Egypt, forming one great state. From here on, Egypt is the two lands, Upper

and Lower Egypt, and the pharaoh undergoes two installations on the throne, two coronations—one with the crown of Upper Egypt, the other with the crown of Lower Egypt. When one of these kings was buried, the whole court was buried with him.

Now we come to the first of the great pyramids, the Step Pyramid of King Zoser, 2600 B.C. This was built by the great architect Imhotep, and all of the motifs of later architecture in Egypt are stated here. They have suddenly come to form. The earlier graves were covered by earth mounds which washed away with time. The Sphinx represents the power of pharaonic rule. Every king is an incarnation of this power. The Sphinx is the son of the lion goddess Sekmet by a strange moon-like god called Ptah, who is usually represented as a mummy. A moonbeam impregnated the goddess and she gave birth to the Sphinx.

The pharaoh is the incarnation of Osiris. He is protected by the sun hawk Horus, the son of Osiris. After the early dynasties, there was the First Intermediary Period. For a number of dynasties there was nothing but upheaval and destruction. Then the Middle Kingdom comes and that is wiped out by an invasion from Asia known as the invasion of the Hyksos. One theory for the entry of the Jews into Egypt is that they came in at the time of the Hyksos. This is just shortly after the time of Hammurabi. If that were so, however, they would not have been there in the time of Ramses because the Hyksos were thrown out at the time of the founding of the New

Kingdom. These are the great dynasties of which we mostly read.

And now I want to give the basic myth of Osiris and Isis. This is the heaven goddess, Nut. Just the opposite of the way it is in Mesopotamia, where the god is above and the goddess is the earth, here we have the heaven goddess, Nut, spangled with stars and here is her consort, Hem, the earth god. This is the lord of the cosmic abyss out of which all has come. Riding on the sky boat, the great boat of Ra, the god of the sun, the souls that are in this barge course over the sky and instead of descending they enter the mouth of Nut and then are born in the east. The lord of air separates heaven and earth. These are basic mythic motifs that will occur in many other mythologies. Now the first children of Hem and Nut are Isis and Osiris. The goddess Isis is the throne on which the pharaoh sits. Osiris is her twin brother. They are husband and wife. The younger brother and sis-

ter are Set and Neftis. They are also husband and wife. Now, in a famous night, Osiris slept with Neftis, thinking she was Isis. This is inattention to details, and from things of that kind bad results can follow. She bore a child, Anubis, who had the head of a jackal.

Set didn't like this, and he planned revenge. He took measurements of Osiris and had a sarcophagus fashioned that would fit him exactly. A jolly party was in full progress when Set comes in and says he has a beautiful sarcophagus and anyone whom it fits can have it. So, like Cinderella and the glass slipper, they all try the sarcophagus. And when Osiris is in it, it fits perfectly, and seventy-two attendants come rushing in, clamp the lid on the sarcophagus, wrap iron bands around it, and throw it into the Nile. Osiris floats down the Nile and is washed ashore in Syria and a great tree grows around the sarcophagus.

Isis starts out to find her husband. She comes to the place in Syria where Osiris is enclosed in the tree. Meanwhile the prince of that little town has had a child. A little boy has been born and the prince has built a palace. The wonderful aroma that comes from this tree has so entranced him that he has had the tree cut down and made into a pillar in the palace. And so Osiris is in the palace, inside a pillar.

Isis is sitting by the well where the young women from the palace come to draw water, and they invite this beautiful older woman in to become nurse for the newborn little prince. She accepts the job and nurses the child from her little finger. Goddesses can stoop only so far.

At night, to give the child immortality, Isis places him in the fireplace and recites her charms. The fire is supposed to burn off his mortal character and turn him into an immortal. Meanwhile, she turns into a swallow and, twittering mournfully, flies around the pillar. Well, one evening the little boy's mother happens to break in on this scene, and as you can imagine, she lets out a scream. There's her baby in the fireplace and there's nobody watching him, there's just a funny twittering swallow flying around a post. And the child has to be rescued from the fire because the spell is broken, and the swallow turns into the beautiful nursemaid. So Isis explains the situation as well as she can, and then she says, "By the way, my husband's in that pillar. Could you please give me the pillar so I can take my husband home." And the king, very polite, says, "Here you are, my darling."

The pillar's put on a barge, and on the way back to the papyrus swamp, Isis takes off the sarcophagus lid, lies upon the dead Osiris, and conceives

Horus. Now Osiris has two sons: one by Neftis—Anubis, the jackal boy, and another by Isis—Horus.

Isis is afraid to go back to the palace because Set has assumed the throne. She goes into the papyrus swamp and gives birth to Horus. The gods Amon and Thot come to assist her.

Meanwhile Set, who is out hunting, follows a boar into the papyrus swamp and finds Isis with Osiris's corpse beside her. In a rage, he tears Osiris into fifteen pieces, scatters the fifteen pieces over the landscape, and poor Isis has to go hunt for him again. She's helped now by Neftis and Anubis, who sniffs around, and they find fourteen of the pieces.

The dead Osiris is associated with the rising of the Nile, which fertilizes Egypt. And the juices of Osiris's disintegrating body are identified with the waters of the Nile. It is he, therefore, who is the fertilizing force of Egypt.

The fourteen pieces are put together and Anubis, in the role later assumed by the priests, embalms Osiris. The missing piece, the genital organs, has been swallowed by a fish. This is the origin of the fish meal on Fridays; it's a sacramental consuming of the sacred flesh.

Osiris, no longer being a generator, is the image of the dead pharaoh and he becomes the lord of the underworld. The resurrected Osiris is now the judge of the dead. His son Horus, who has rapidly grown up, has engaged in a great battle with his uncle Set to avenge his father. In that battle, Horus lost an eye. This eye is symbolic of sacrificial offering. Through the loss of that eye he brought his father back to life. Set lost a testicle in the combat.

So now we come to the judgment scene, from the Book of the Dead of Ani. Here is Osiris seated on the throne of the judge of the dead, by the waters of eternal life. Behind him are his two queens, Isis and Neftis. He has the symbolic shepherd's crook

and the winnowing whip, which winnows wheat, separating the chaff from the seed. We see the eye of Horus by which he has been resurrected, and growing from the waters of eternal life is the lotus of the world with the four sons of Horus, who represent the four points of the compass of the universe. When a person dies, he becomes identified with Osiris. This is a very important theme. The dead person is called Osiris. Osiris Jones, let's say. He goes on the underworld journey to unite with Osiris. Osiris is going to Osiris. I and the father are one, that motif. On the way, he eats back all the gods. This means that the gods are understood to be projections of the energies of ourselves. We consume the gods. In some cases it's represented actually as cannibalism. In other ways, other texts, he might simply say, "My head is the head of Anubis. My shoulders are the shoulders of Set." That is to say, every organ of my body is the organ of some god and nobody will take my heart from me in the underworld. You get some sense of the dangers of the underworld. "Get you back, you crocodile of the north. Get you back, you crocodile of the south." Then he comes to the great moment of the opening of the mouth in the underworld: "I am yesterday, today, and tomorrow. I have the power to be born a second time. I am that source from which the gods arise." This is a great realization. This is what must be realized—properly before you die, but if not, then on the way to the underworld.

Next, in the underworld we come to the great weighing of the heart of the dead against a feather. If the heart is heavier than a feather, a monster will consume the man. If the feather is heavier than the heart or of the same balance, then the person is eligible for spiritual life. Ani, the scribe for whom this papyrus was prepared, is being conducted to the weighing. Anubis does the weighing, and the monster is waiting to see if he can have a meal. Thot records the results. Finally, under the charge of Horus, Ani is led to the very throne of Osiris. This is a book of the dead and the mythology is explicit.

Now we come to an extraordinary man, Akhnaton. The dates of his reign are 1377 to 1358 B.C. He's said to have been the first monotheist. That's wrong. I regard him as the first Protestant. He rejects the ceremonialism, the ritualism of the Theban priesthood, which had gained enormous wealth. Priesthoods always do, as long as they survive. He rejects the priestly orders of thieves and founds a city of his own, Amarna, in the desert. His idea was that the deities should not be imaged, and he presents as the symbol of deity, the solar disk. Instead of Amon, who is the lord creator of the Theban system, he calls the deity Aton, which actually is the reanimation of a much earlier notion.

Sigmund Freud suggested in his *Moses and Monotheism* that Moses had been an officer in the court of Akhnaton and that it was probably one of Akhnaton's daughters who had pulled Moses out of the water in the little basket of rushes. With the collapse of Akhnaton's court in Amarna—when he died the whole thing was wiped out —Moses, who was a believing minister in the court, picked up a group of working people in the delta area and left Egypt with them to continue this monotheistic cult. But the difference between Akhnaton's so-called monotheism and that of Moses is that Akhnaton saw this mystery represented in the solar disk as informing all the gods and mythologies of the whole Near East. You are the one who appears as so-and-so here, so-and-so there. But

the Yahwehist monotheism says, "There is no other God in the world. Those others are devils." So this is a total distinction which has to be recognized if you're going to understand what's going on.

The symbols of Akhnaton's lordship were again the shepherd's crook of the good shepherd who guards and guides his flock and the winnowing whip for separating the chaff from the seed. This is the discipline and this the protection, the two aspects of rule— the god of mercy and the god of justice.

Akhnaton's beautiful queen was Nefertiti. Almost every woman I know who believes in reincarnation thinks she was Nefertiti at one time. I was actually in Egypt with one of those ladies. When we were in Karnak she would say, "That's all so familiar." Here are Akhnaton, Nefertiti, and their three beautiful daughters with their artificially deformed heads. We see the solar disk of Aton with its rays

of blessing, each ray terminating in a hand, blessing this dear little family.

Akhnaton had no sons, only three lovely daughters. One of his daughters married the young prince who is called Tutankh-*Amen*. That is to say, as soon as Akhnaton died, the Amon priesthood took over again and the young pharaoh was again of the Amon cult. However, the solar disk and the hands of blessing continued.

The tomb of Tutankhamen is a miserable little tomb in Egyptian terms. It's divided into two, and half was loaded with this gorgeous stuff, just thrown in as though in a junk shop. The reason it was all there was that nobody seems to have thought it worth trying to rob that tomb. Right next door is the tomb of Seti I, which is enormous, and every bit of it is engraved and painted. The art is perfect and it was made never to be seen. There was a kind of reality there, a concretization, that endured. The soul, one aspect of the soul, the ba, remained in the tomb. Tutankhamen's tomb has a very interesting symbolic form. There were three rectangular boxes, one inside the other in the way of Chinese boxes. They were gold plated and there were four lovely guardian spirits watching over them. Within the boxes was a great stone coffin and within that, two sarcophagi. The outer one, in the form of the young pharaoh, was of precious wood inlaid with gold and lapis lazuli. The inner one was of solid gold, again in the form of the pharaoh.

I've noticed many, many parallels between Egyptian symbology and the mystical philosophy of India. I'm just going to offer it as a suggestion that these three boxes, and the two sarcophagi inside the stone coffin, represent what in India are called the five sheaths—the five sheaths that enclose the atman, that enclose the self, the transcendent mystery. Since I'm going to be talking about Hinduism a bit, it is worth speaking of these five sheaths now.

The first sheath is Anamayakosha, food. That's what our body is made of. It's made of food and when you die it becomes food for the worms, the vultures, the jackals, or the fire. The second sheath is Pranamayakosha, breath. The sheath of breath ignites the food, oxidation, burns, gives heat, temperature, and life. The third sheath is Manamayakosha, the mental sheath. Now, this mentality is in touch with the food sheath. And when the food sheath is in pain, it feels pain and thinks, "Oh, all is sorrowful." And when the food sheath is happy, it's happy too. The mental sheath is oriented to the food and breath sheaths. This is what I think is represented in the three rectangular boxes.

Then we have a long gap, and I think this may be what is represented by the stone coffin, or maybe not. Maybe the stone coffin represented the next sheath. But I think more likely the wooden sarcophagus did. The next sheath is known as the Janamayakosha, the sheath of wisdom. This is the wisdom of the body: the wisdom that shaped you in the mother's womb, the wisdom that knew, the moment you were born, how to nurse, the wisdom that brings up the grass and informs the trees and the mountains and universe. The wisdom of the body: that spontaneous thing on which the mentality rides and which the mentality has to know about. We eat breakfast. Our body digests that breakfast. I dare say there isn't a soul who would know mentally what the chemistry of the breakfast requirements were for digestion. And yet you do it. Who else? That's your Wisdom Body.

And then what do you think? Beneath the Wisdom Body, Anandamayakosha, the sheath of bliss. Life is a manifestation of rapture. And this poor mental sheath up here gets all tied up with what's happening to the food body. And it thinks, "Oh dear, oh dear. All life is sorrowful." Suppose every two weeks somebody goes over the lawn with a lawnmower. Suppose the grass were to think, "Well, what's the use?"

These are the two completely different orientations: the mental sheath has to do with ethics, good and evil, light and darkness, pain and pleasure; the wisdom sheath knows that there's something before that. And it's rapture. So, that's what you are really. You're rooted in rapture; and even in your pain, in your great anguish, in your sorrow, if you know where the rapture door is you can realize that this is life's rapture. And where the pain is there's the life. This is the kind of stuff that we have in these heroic mythologies.

If Moses was, as Freud suggests, a member of the court of Akhnaton, then the Exodus must have taken place around 1358 B.C., the death of Akhnaton. That's the earliest date anybody's ever proposed for the Exodus. In the Book of Exodus, the pharaoh, who is impugned there, seems to be Ramses II, whose dates are about 1305 to 1234 or 1236 B.C.. He reigned for a long, long season. He was enormously powerful. I don't think any scholar would suggest that he could possibly have been the pharaoh of the Exodus. Furthermore, he wasn't drowned in the Red Sea. He is entombed at Abu Simbel. There is a great pair of tombs for Ramses and his favorite wife, who was one of his daughters. In George Bernard Shaw's *Caesar and Cleopatra*, when Caesar meets Cleopatra, he has

among his officers a British officer. When he learns from Cleopatra that she was born from an incestuous marriage, the British officer expresses great shock. Caesar says to Cleopatra, "Don't mind him. He's British. He thinks that the laws of his tribe are the laws of the universe."

This great tomb, because of the ridiculous Aswan Dam, has been elevated and placed up above the waters by a miracle of modern engineering.

The horrible thing about the dam is that Lake Nasser backed up and wiped out the whole province of Nubia. And where are the Nubians? They are packed into miserable housing developments nearby.

When I saw that, I thought of Goethe's *Faust*, part II, act V. Faust has won the world war, and he's now going to make the world great. And what is he doing? He is draining swamps and building housing devel-

opments. But in order to build the housing development, he has to displace people who were there in the first place. Baucis and Philemon, a lovely little old couple, are living in their ancestral home. When they are displaced by a couple of rough thugs, they die. And this is it, for the whole province of Nubia.

This fantastic tomb was carved with little pick-axes into the mountain. The date would be that of the death of Ramses, around 1234 or 1236 B.C. What great art! When you get over the distance, the form is perfect. In the representation of Ramses, he has the shepherd's crook and the winnowing whip, a standard motif in Egyptian art of the conquering pharaoh. The enemy is on his knees and the pharaoh has hold of his top knot and is about to slam him dead. These are conquering people.

After the Hyksos invaded Egypt

around 1750 B.C. and were then driven out, the Egyptians became imperialists. They moved up through Palestine and Asia Minor as far as what is now Turkey, to where the Hittites, the children of Hit, came in. And there they were stopped. And so you have the great Egyptian empire as a reply to the invasion that had taken place.

At Abu Simbel, side by side with Horus, Amon, and Ptah, is Ramses himself. So, Ramses is now among the highest deities.

With respect to the Exodus again, during the time of Akhnaton, who wasn't paying much attention to the empire, letters were coming, written in Babylonian, to the court at Amarna. Known as the Amarna letters, they were from the governors of the various provinces in Asia, complaining that their provinces were being invaded by Bedouins from the desert who were sometimes called Haberu. This is certainly the first appearance of the word in writing. These were tribes of the kind that are associated with the Mosaic history. So there were invasions taking place at the time of Akhnaton. Yet the Exodus is generally associated in the biblical tradition with the time of Ramses II, which was very much later. But nobody can possibly believe that anything like that happened at the time of Ramses. Another pharaoh,

Merneptah, ruled from about 1234 to 1220 B.C. He was a weak pharaoh, actually physically ill, and he died very young. If there was anything like the Exodus, he may have been the pharaoh then.

Now we come to this amusing problem of crossing the waters of the Red Sea. Is this to be interpreted as a mythological event, as a spiritual symbol of some kind, or is it a fact? I have many friends who say that they crossed in a shallow place and the wind was blowing from just the right direction and so they got across. Read on a few more chapters, and we come to the Jordan. The waters of the Jordan pile up like walls on either side and the tribe again walks between. This is a mythological motif you'll find everywhere, the crossing of the waters. It's comparable to the Symplegades, the rocks that clash together. The pair of opposites have withdrawn and we've gone through the middle.

What came into Egypt? The patriarchs. Joseph, through the well, was the first—mythological again. It was a dry well, but it was a well just the same. So we come in through water and we go out through water. When you have this in and out in a mythology, try to see what came in and what went out and then you'll find what the mystical value is. What came in were the patriarchs; what went out were the people. That is a great thing that coalesced and came to knowledge of itself in Egypt, in the land of suffering, in the abyss. Moses was not the hero. The hero of the Old Testament is the people. They are conceived of as a unit, and one is a member of that people or one is out. The accent is on the group, the group, the group. Membership in the group is entirely Near Eastern. In Europe you get another accent. Now, one of the problems in the European assimilation of Christianity was recovering and maintaining the sense of the individual as a unique entity—the translation of this group tradition into a tradition of individual realization. This is the problem of the Grail tradition in the thirteenth century in Europe. This is when it was pulled together in a new way.

This struck me when I was teaching at Sarah Lawrence. More than half of my students were Jewish girls. One young woman, who had been one of the most remarkable members of her class, said to me, "You know, Mr. Campbell, if I didn't think of myself as Jewish, I wouldn't know my identity." I was stunned. I said, "Rachel, what are you saying? I never thought of you as Jewish or anything else, but as Rachel. Suppose I were to say to you, 'If I didn't think of myself as Irish, I wouldn't know my identity.' That wouldn't make sense, would it?"

These are two totally different ways of relating to race. One is "Oh, yes, that's what I am and all my peculiarities come from that misfortune." The other is "No, this is my own being." This is important to realize about the Jewish tradition. It has its roots here in the idea of a people.

At the next meeting Martin Buber was talking about the Phoenicians and what terrible criminals they were in sacrificing their older sons to Moloch. About fifteen minutes later he comes to Abraham about to sacrifice Isaac. Well, you can't let a thing like that go by and I raised my hand. He looked at me a little more cautiously than the first time, and I said, "Dr. Buber, how do you distinguish between a divine and a diabolical invitation?" He said, "What do you mean by that?" I said, "Well, only fifteen minutes ago you were excoriating the Phoenicians for killing their oldest sons and now you're celebrating Abraham for having been about to do the same thing with his oldest son. So what is the answer?" Dr. Buber said, "The answer is We"— that's a capital W—"We believe that God spoke to Abraham." That's all I got from that man.

So things that are done by us are different from things that are done by others and that's another characteristic of our whole tradition. Moses is not the hero. The tribe is the hero. Ours is a tribal mythology, and the only god of the universe is ours. This is very important.

What about the plagues and all that kind of thing? What kind of deity is that? He sends these plagues for the fun of it; he hardens pharaoh's heart so that he won't let the people go so he can send another plague. This is what it says in the book, which is a good thing to read, you know.

Just at the time of Akhnaton, 1377 to 1358 B.C. or so, the Indo-Europeans are invading India. This is the beginning of a total transformation of the Indian consciousness. These are nomads, and from here on I want to discuss the emergence of the philosophies and ritual cults of India. We will then move on to more recent matters.

5

The Sacred Source:
The Perennial Philosophy of the East

I first want to present a couple of simple ideas. The first, which I've discussed many times, is an idea of the German anthropologist Adolf Bastian. He recognized that throughout the mythologies and religious systems of the world, the same images, the same themes are constantly recurring, appearing everywhere. He called these "Elementary Ideas," *Elementargedanken*. But he recognized also that wherever they occurred, they appeared in different costumes with different applications and different interpretations. He called these provincial differences "Folk Ideas," or "Ethnic Ideas"—*Volkgedanken*. Now this is a very important distinction. It divides our subject into two quite different departments. Historians and ethnologists are interested in the differences, and one can study the mythologies and the philosophies of the world with an accent on these differences. On the other hand, the problem emerges of the Elementary Ideas. Why are they everywhere? This is a psychological problem, and it's a problem that separates us in our discussion of comparative forms from the whole research having to do with differences. Now in giving the story of the Oriental systems, I want to insist on the elementary aspect.

The second idea that I have in mind is as follows. Somewhere in the ninth and eighth centuries B.C. a shift of accent takes place, particularly in the Orient. Instead of simply presenting the images, the images are interpreted. That is to say, there was a turn from visual and active relationship to the forms of myth—through the imagery of myth and the rituals through which the myth is rendered into life—and a turn to thinking about these things, interpreting them. And so the Oriental philosophies actually represent a discourse interpreting the elementary ideas.

Now, what happened in the West, following the period of Aristotle, in particular, was a gradual attack on the mythological ideas, so that criticism in the West tended to separate itself from the elementary ideas. However, there is an undercurrent throughout Western thinking also. It's associated with Gnosticism, alchemy, and many of the discredited manners of thought that carry on this interest in what

might be called the perennial philosophy. I'm thinking of Perennial Philosophy as expounded by Ananda K. Coomaraswamy and picked up by Aldous Huxley in his *The Perennial Philosophy*. I'm thinking of this as the translation into verbal discourse of the implications of the mythic images. And that's why there can be found in the mystical philosophies throughout the world the same ideas recurring. The continuities that we can recognize in myth come over into philosophy. This is what is known as the perennial philosophy.

Myth comes in the same zone as dream, and this is the zone of what I would call the Wisdom Body. When you go to sleep, it's the body that's talking. What the body is moved by are energies that it does not control. These are the energies that control the body. They come in from the great biological ground. They are there. They are energies and they are manners of consciousness. But we also have in this body this affair of the head, and it has a system of thinking on its own. There's a whole manner of consciousness that stems from the head-set, and it is different in its knowledge from that of the body. When a baby is born, it knows just what to do with its mother's body. It is ready for the environment into which it is put. It doesn't have to be instructed, these things happen. This is the work of the Wisdom Body. That same wisdom brought the little thing into form in its mother's body. It was shaped by these energies that live in us, and of which we are the carnal manifestation. This wisdom of the dream, wisdom of the vision, is the wisdom then of the perennial philosophy. When you dream, your waking consciousness aspect does not understand the dream, and so you have to go to a psychoanalyst, who doesn't understand it either. The interpretation is gradual and it comes from an exploration, by the head, of your own wisdom. And so we find that there is a kind of radical distinction between the perennial philosophy in its mode and its axioms, quite differ-

ent from the axioms and mode of the rational system.

The interpretation of the mythic forms went forward in great style, principally in India, very early. And so it's through reviewing the mythologies and the interpretations of the myths in India and then in China and Japan that I propose to introduce us to what I take to be the ground thinking of the perennial philosophy. While I want to give a sense of the richness and wonder of the ethnic aspect of the Oriental systems, my principal interest is in extracting from them the elementary—not accenting the ethnic but extracting the elementary.

Here we are on the Ganges. The idea of the sacred river, the Jordan, the

waters that pour from heaven, becomes translated into the idea of the grace of the divine, flowing inexhaustibly out of some source. In India the very source of the Ganges, up in the Himalayan area, is a very sacred place. If one goes there, there are yogis all around practicing yoga, getting close to the source, literally.

The main problem with symbols is that people tend to get lost in the symbol. So they think they have to go up to the head of the Ganges in order to get to the source. The problem in myth, the problem in mysticism, is that you should not lose the message in the symbol. The message always is of the spirit, and when the symbol is taken to be the fact, so that you have to go to Haridwar in order to get to the source of the Ganges, you've mistaken the message.

There's a similar mistake made in the notion that you have to go to Israel to get to the Promised Land. This concretization is one of the major deceptions in the Western handling of symbols. It's one of the reasons why we've lost touch with the elementary idea and the perennial messages—the concretization of the symbol, the notion, for example, that God is a fact. The God idea is a symbol. Anything that can be named and regarded as a form is a symbol.

There's a wonderful saying by Gerhart Hauptmann, the German writer, "Dichten heisst, hinter Worten das Urwort erklingen lasse." ("Writing poetry consists in letting the Word be heard behind words.") The whole world is of symbols. In Goethe's words, "Alles Vergangliche ist nur ein Gleichnis." ("Everything that is transitory is but a reference.") But the reference isn't to any thing. It's to what is called the void, *sunya*, and it's called the void because no thought can reach it. So what these symbols are talking about is something that can't be talked about. They have to become transparent. They have to open. What we find then is that the ethnic opens to the elementary. One of our problems—and these are the two great sources, now, of the problem here in Western interpretation of these matters—is the Aristotelian accent on rational thinking and the biblical focus on the ethnic reference of the mythic symbol. These two pin us down to the world of facts and rational cogitation. But from this other standpoint, those are exactly what have to be transcended; they have to be rendered transparent and not opaque. So I'm going to try to see the whole Hindu system in that way and by comparison refer over to our Western themes.

Take the idea of the Jordan and baptism, bathing, going into the river, partaking of the grace. One has to ac-

company the act with a meditation on its sense. Then consider the idea of the sacred city, the city at the sacred place where the grace flows, a city such as Benares, the city of Siva, who is probably the oldest worshiped god in the high culture systems of the world. Benares is Siva's city. It is a fantastic mess, just a jungle of temples of all kinds. And people come there to die because—a literal reading of the symbol—when you are close to the Ganges, you are close to the divine grace. And it's only a short step then to heaven. So we find them making themselves sick, you might say, by bathing in this filthy water. Only a little bit up the way they are burning bodies and throwing them into the Ganges, which is a good place to go— reading the symbol literally again.

The whole idea of pilgrimage is translating into a literal, physical act the pilgrimage of moving into the center of your own heart. It's good to make a pilgrimage if, while doing so, you meditate on what you are doing and know that it's into your inward life that you are moving.

At the ghat, the people bathe in the Ganges. It's a constant, as it were, baptism rite; going in and absorbing the virtue of this miraculous gift of the universe, the waters of the Ganges. The Ganges actually is a goddess, Ganga, and this flowing water is the grace that comes to us from the power of the female power. In Joyce's *Finnegans Wake,* he uses the same image for the River Liffey, which flows through Dublin, and Dublin on the Liffey is precisely the counterpart of Benares on the Ganges. The whole secret of relating mythology and the spiritual life to your environment is here involved. It is called *land-nam* by the people in Iceland, land-claiming through naming the landscape. You read the land that you are living in as the holy land.

In a very interesting letter in the *New York Times,* a young Jewish boy protested the idea of having to be thought of as being in the Diaspora, having left the Holy Land. He said, "My country, my land, is here in the United States. And I have not been forced to be here, and it's my choice and pleasure to name this my Holy Land." I thought this was a wonderful statement of the problem that we have in disengaging ourselves from what might be called "traditional inheritance," which tends to concretize its own symbol system. He had released himself and found the whole sense of the holy land in his own place. And so Joyce does this with the river and the city; his holy land, you might say, was Dublin, as perhaps ours is New York on the Hudson. But we've so secularized the idea that one even gets a laugh thinking of the Hudson as a gift of divine grace.

This bathing place goes back four thousand years. It is at Mohenjo-Daro in the Indus Valley. Mohenjo-Daro is one of a little cluster of small cities, one of the two largest that emerge in India about 2000 B.C. We come now to the historical matter. Already, in this Indus Valley civilization, also called the Dravidian civilization, also called the Mohenjo-Daro civilization, also called the Harappa civilization—you see, names don't matter, they're but a reference—we have the emergence of a culture of the style of ancient Crete and Mesopotamia. It is contemporary with those worlds, 2000 B.C. And one of the most important buildings in this ruined city is a public bath. It's assumed that this had religious meaning or value, and that a continuity from

that is what we meet when we come to the Ganges. It's a continuous thing for four thousand years, the sacred water, the bathing in the sacred water.

Benares is deep in India, as we come in from the west. In Mesopotamia, on the rivers Tigris and Euphrates the first city-civilizations of the world appear, around 3500 B.C. It's becoming clearer and clearer that all of the high civilizations of the world are reflections from this source. Around 3500 B.C. in Mesopotamia, 2500 B.C. in the Indus area, 1500 B.C. with the Shang dynasty in China, and then it jumps the ocean. In Mexico and Peru we have the Olmec (1100–800 B.C.) and Chavín (900–200 B.C.) phenomena. It's out of these that the high-civilization systems come. When we speak of high

civilizations, we speak of a civilization in which there is writing (except in one case), developed mathematics, and extreme attention to the cycles of the planets through the constellations.

This cycling of the planets through the constellations is the great critical factor in the transformation of consciousness at this time. Because of writing and because of mathematics, it became possible to make records, precise records, of the passage of the planets through the constellations. In Mesopotamia, as early as 3200 B.C. apparently, it became evident that the planets were moving at a mathematically predictable rate. And the notion of a cosmic order, the order of the cosmos, comes into expression. When people talk about mythology and rituals, they usually talk about it from the standpoint of modern mentality. They speak about finding the causes of the world, origin myths, and so on: explanatory myths, what are called etiological myths. That's not what myths are about. Myths do not have to do with analyzing and scientifically discovering causes. Myth has to do with relating the human being to his environment. And before the discovery of these great planetary movements, this was largely the environment of the animal and plant worlds.

So the very early mythologies have to do with relating to the animal world. The problem is that the animal is respected, but the animal is nevertheless killed and eaten. The problem of recognizing what might be called the covenant between the animal world and the human world and recognizing the miracle of life which lives by killing and eating life is a major problem that has to be solved—relating the mind to this act of continually killing and consuming animals and wearing their skins or living in tents made of them. That's one aspect.

The other is the plant world. Again, you are killing and eating life. Both the animal and the plant are like the river Ganges, pouring into the world for your sustenance, and so they are revered. They become the revered powers and symbols to which man must relate himself.

But then comes this discovery of the great cycles of the heavens, and what you find is a great concern to relate the whole organization of the society to this cycling—a tremendous accent on seasonal festivals. These festivals are not meant to control nature. They are meant to put you in accord with nature, and when you are in accord with nature, nature will yield its bounty. This is something that is coming up in our own consciousness now, in the ecology movement's recognizing that by violating the environment in which we are living we are really cutting off the energy and the source of our own living. It's through this sense of accord, living properly in relation to what has to be done in this world, that one fosters the vitality of the environment.

So there you have this business of accord with the natural world. Well, when the great cosmic order was discovered, the problem of coming into accord with that becomes the high system. And we have an echo of it in the prayer, "Thy will be done on earth as it is in heaven." The heavenly signs became the signs of the order of the great spiritual world. Now, of course, we are moving past that since we're sending rockets up there and men have walked on the moon, which was the first spiritual light, you might say. What we are learning is that the separation of spirit and earth has been transcended, that these two, in some sense, are much more one than the dualism of our inherited philosophy would suggest.

At the time of the emergence of the high civilizations in the river valleys, there were ranging in the great grazing plains of southern Europe nomadic cattle-herding people, the Indo-Europeans, or Aryans. We now turn to the role of these people in India. These are the Vedic Aryans. They came into India, Persia, and Europe.

There was a great spiritual crisis in India after the arrival of the Indo-Europeans. This is when we begin to translate myth into philosophy. The sacred books of India, the fundamental sacred books, are known as the Vedas, which are a collection of hymns. The word *veda* is from a Sanskrit root, *vid*, which means "knowledge." The Vedas are the manifestations of knowledge, and the knowledge is a specific kind of knowledge. It's called *sruti*, which means "heard." The Rhishis, or saints, were people who did not invent the poems, the hymns, of the Vedas. They heard them, just as anyone who listens to the muse will hear. You can write either out of your own intention or out of inspiration. There is such a thing. It comes up and talks. Those who have heard deeply the rhythms and hymns and words of the gods can recite those hymns in such a way that the gods will be attracted. The Vedas form the substance of the rituals by which the powers of nature, personified as gods, are invoked to the support of the intentions of the Aryan society. You invoke the gods to do your will. And so the characteristic leadership of these tribes is one of a warrior leader, and the other of a magician, of a Rhishi, who can invoke the gods. So we have two kinds of power going. These are the twin heroes.

You have a similar thing in the early

part of Exodus—Moses and Aaron, the warrior chief and the priest. At a certain important moment, the warrior chief had the higher revelation. He went up on Mount Sinai, and the god with the horns of light spoke to him a new message. When he came down there was poor Aaron still worshiping bulls, the old symbol of the cycle of time. And Moses then gets angry, breaks the laws, goes back, gets a second edition, and comes back again. There then takes place a very interesting ritual. He grinds up the golden bull and mixes it with water and makes everybody take a communion meal. Did you ever notice that? That's what happens. And from then on, of course, Aaron is out, and Moses is in the two roles. So out of that tradition we have the same kind of theme that comes with the caliphs of the Islamic world. The spiritual ruler and the political ruler are the same ruler. These two things are brought very closely together, so that spirit and society are very closely united.

The hymns invoke the gods and then the altars are set up for the rituals. Now, for a settled people it's possible to worship in terms of the place where you live. This particular grove is a sacred grove, and we go there to get the inspiration of the powers of nature that are experienced there. Or this pond, or this particular old tree, or this strange, interesting rock is sacred. But when you are a nomadic people, your worship has to be to that which is everywhere. Now the Hebrews had the ark, which is, in anthropological language, a fetish that's carried about with the divine power in it. The Hindus and the Aryans worshiped the sun, which is seen everywhere, and the powers of the winds, the clouds, the broad-spreading earth. They would set up their altars as symbolic representations of the nature of the universe, that is, of the order and form of the universe. Then they would invoke the deities who would come, as it were, sitting around like birds on the trees waiting to be fed, because they were going to have a shared feast. Agni, the god of fire, would be the mouth of the gods, and the offerings would be poured into the fire. Then Agni would take them, as a mother bird takes a worm, and feed all the gods. So this little social, invisible society is to be thought of. The Greeks were doing the same thing. They also were Aryans. They also had their altars and priests and rituals and offerings and so forth and so on.

So those were the Vedas. The Vedas were not turned into writing for many, many centuries. They were known orally and communicated orally. In the form that we now have them, they date from about 1000 B.C. That's the first stage. That's the stage of myth and ritual.

Then comes a set of books (and now here's the big turning point) known as the Brāhmanas, the books of the Brāhmans. The first *a* in Brāhman is a long *a*, and it means "related to." The Brāhmans are the priests and they are related to Brahman, without a long *a*. It's a neuter noun and it means "brrrr," energy. That's the divine energy, the Brahman. Brahman is no deity; deities are personifications of aspects of Brahman. So are you and so is the world. The Brāhmans are those who are in touch with the energy of Brahman. They go to work to interpret the meaning of the sacrifice. The Brāhmanas are very dreary books to read. They are pedantic discussions of the sacrifice, what it consists of, what the different ladles are like, and so forth and so on. But it comes to this final point, "What is the nature of the sacrifice?" It's terribly important because through the sacrifice we influence the gods. The sacrifice is stronger than the gods. But who operates the sacrifice? The Brāhmans. Therefore, the Brāhmans are stronger than the gods. Therefore, an

fire. So he speaks with the voice of the fire. We get the same thing from Jesus, five hundred to six hundred years later, where he identifies himself with the fire, with the Christ energy that supports all beings, and speaks out of that. He doesn't speak as Jesus of Nazareth, born of Mary. He speaks as the twice-born, the one who has taken birth, the virgin birth, of the recognition of the spiritual life which is his true life. And so we have the gurus.

Now this period is a fascinating one. It's a period of enormous transformations. In Persia there is a great teacher at this time, Zoroaster, or Zarathustra. The Gathas, or hymns, of Zoroaster are so close to Sanskrit that the Persians and Aryans of India cannot have been long separated when these were written. The languages were too close. The probable dating of Zoroaster is somewhere around the time of the Upanishads. It's out of the Zoroastrian message that our whole Western tradition comes, in contrast to that which is of the Buddha.

Zoroaster was totally against sacrifice. He was totally against the whole drift of these psychologies in India and of the earlier mythologies that were concerned with putting yourself in harmony with the universe. Zoroaster, in his mythology, sees two gods: Ahura Mazda, the Lord of Light, after whom the Mazda bulbs were named—

Ahura means "kind of spirit," and Mazda is this particular spirit of light —who is all light, all benevolence, all power, all knowledge; and against him, the opposite deity, Angra Mainyu, who is darkness, hypocrisy, and deception. What Zoroaster has done is concretize two opposites; the good and the evil, the light and the dark have been personified—overpersonified, you might say—as gods.

The mythology is as follows. The good god created a good world which was all light, consequently invisible. To see something you have to have shadow. Angra Mainyu, who is always late and always jealous, is angry at seeing this and decides to do something about it. He pours darkness and sin and everything nasty into it. So there is a fall, and the universe consists of the good and the evil power in conflict and in union.

Do not put yourself in harmony with the universe. That's exactly what you mustn't do. That's what you are in the first place. You are a mixture. You must through intention, through decision, through action, and through courage align yourself with what you recognize as the good.

Then the myth tells that there came into the world a savior to teach the way to accent the good. As a result of the action of this savior, there is now taking place a restoration. There are the good people who are restoring the world to its original condition, so that you have a straight line ascent to a restoration. There will come a time when the crisis will occur, when all darkness will be wiped out. There will be a second-coming of the savior, in the form of a figure known as Saoshyant, and darkness will be permanently eliminated, the Lord of Darkness himself eliminated. There will be nothing but light again.

Do you recognize the story? So we have on the West Coast this Western side of the story, this idea of "Don't put yourself in accord with nature. Fix nature up."

We move now over to the Buddhist side. The Buddha is saying, "Yes, all life is sorrowful. That's the nature of life. Good and evil. All these names that you give things, that which is 'good' and that which is 'evil,' it's all mixed. And that's the way it is." The Buddha used, actually, the terminology of a Hindu medical man. A medical man comes in and observes a patient.

"What's wrong with the patient?"

"The patient is suffering."

"Is there a cure for suffering?"

"All life is suffering, there is a cure for suffering."

"The cure for suffering, what is the cure?"

"Nirvana."

"What is the healthy state? Now what is Nirvana?"

There are many ways of getting this wrong. Nirvana consists in the psychological stance that makes you indifferent to suffering. What is it that turns your life into nothing but suffering? It is desire and fear—desire for something, some delusory desire, and fear lest you should lose something. When this desire and fear are quenched, you come to what is known as the Mahasukha, the great delight, the realization of rapture. When you are experiencing rapture, the pain doesn't hurt. It's that getting into a center that gives you such a participation in the rapture of the process. You are right in the center and are neither winning nor losing. You are in being. This is Nirvana.

Now there were many people talking about Nirvana in the Buddha's time. One of the great groups were the Jains. Jainism goes back—almost undoubtedly to the Indus Valley—and is extremely physical in its notion of achieving nirvanic release. The essential idea in Jainism is that the soul, what is called "Jiva," the living monad, is infected with action, which is called "karma," which blackens and renders heavy the luminous Jiva. Now, they don't try to say how it happened. All they are saying is this is the way it is. The goal of their yoga is to clean out the black, clean out action. How do they do it? By sitting, Mulabanda, all senses closed, not active, but you're breathing still. So the problem with the Jains is to die not one moment before you have become completely released from the desire to live. It's harder than you think to get to not to want to live.

And so the Jain community is of two groups: one, the secular group, the lay community, individuals who hope that in a number of incarnations they will be ready for the next act; and the other, the monks and nuns, who have already cut themselves off from life and are, as it were, dead. They are trying to die. The first step, of course —even the lay people take this step— is to become vegetarians. This is saying "No" to the way life is. "We don't kill and eat animals." But you're killing and eating plants. The Jains recognize that, too, so there's another step, where you don't kill and eat plants, either. You wait for them to die. That's a nice supper for you. You do not pick an apple from a tree. You wait for it really to be dead and fall. Also, you are very careful about drinking water at night, lest there be a little bug in it or something. There are very few Jains left, naturally. In Bombay, where most Jains remain, you see people walking with a sort of surgeon's mask over their mouths so that they won't breathe in bugs. There was a very amusing custom in the old days in Bombay. Two chaps with a bed full of bedbugs would walk through the town saying, "Who will feed the bugs, who will feed the bugs?" They were being generous to life. Now, I don't know why you want to foster life and kill your own, but all religions have a point of absurdity in them. Well, a lady would then throw a coin out of the window, and one of these two chaps would lie in the bed and become a grazing ground for the bedbugs. He gets the coin and she gets the merit.

On the other hand, you yourself are trying not to eat, and the first thing to do is limit the number of steps you take in a day. With every step, you press down on the ground and probably kill some little thing that's got its little dwelling underneath. So the days are gradually reduced to sitting where you are and not eating. And then, of course, it happens. The Buddha said, "No, no, no." He said that this is reading the whole thing physically. What you must die to is, psychologically, your desires and your fears. And then, in a very interesting way, life becomes positive.

6

The Way to Enlightenment:
Buddhism

The Buddha's dates are 563 to 483 B.C. This is a long time back. I want to stress the date 500 B.C., which is, as we'll see a little later on, of great importance. In the first centuries of Buddhist art, the Buddha himself was never represented, because he had already escaped from his body. Here he appears as a tree. His body was there, but his presence was like the sun that has set. He had left the body behind like a sunset. It wasn't there. However, five hundred years later we begin to have images of the Buddha, which means another kind of Buddhism has come into expression.

The first order of Buddhism was very strongly monastic. As I've said with respect to Jainism, the community hopes in later incarnations to be able to renounce the world, to quit the world and to go on the quest for nirvanic release. Early Buddhism carried this message also. It was very strongly monastic. But then, in the first century

A.D., in northwest India, the idea changed. There's another Buddhism. The first century A.D. was the first century of Christianity as well—only a short distance to the west.

The first Buddhism is called Theravada. *Vaāda* means "the word," and *thera* means "of the saints"—the doctrine of the old saints. Another name for this Buddhism is Hinayana. *Yana* means "ferryboat," and *hina* means "little." So we have little ferryboat Buddhism. Only a very few people can ride in a little ferryboat—those who have said "No" to life. They are going to nirvana. But the whole sense of nirvanic realization is that you have transcended pairs of opposites: desire and fear, you and me. We've gone to unity. So the distinction between samsara, suffering in the world, and nirvana, or rapture in transcendence, is that there's no distinction. So now we can begin to see that the world itself is a manifestation of Buddha consciousness.

The images of the Buddha, which begin to appear five or six hundred years after the Buddha's death, have nothing to do with that beautiful character of 500 B.C. One of the earliest images of the Buddha we have is in Ceylon. He's seated on the ground, which means this is a man who through meditation has identified his consciousness with Buddha consciousness, the transcendent consciousness, which lives in all beings.

There's a wonderful story in a paper by Daisetz Suzuki. The young student said to his master, "Am I in possession of Buddha consciousness?" The master said, "No." The student said, "Well, I've been told that all things are in the possession of Buddha consciousness. The rocks, the trees, the butterflies, the birds, the animals, all beings." The master said, "You are correct. All things are in possession of Buddha consciousness. The rocks, the trees, the butterflies, the bees, the birds, the animals, all beings—but not you." "Not me? Why not?" "Because you are asking this question."

If you've put your identification of yourself with this rational problem, you are not getting the message. The Buddha is one who wiped that out, got the message, and now is living out of the message.

Here we have the Buddha on a lotus. This is the Buddha as manifestation. This wonderful posture is known as earth-touching. The lotus, like the water of the Ganges, is a manifestation of the grace of the eternal life pouring into the world. That's what the rose represents in medieval symbolism in the Christian tradition. The image of the Trinity appears on the celestial rose. The image of the Buddha appears on the celestial lotus. When you

have a figure seated on the lotus, or on the rose, it is a personification of the energy already represented in that flower. So the Buddha didn't have to work at all to realize his identity.

There are two ways of thinking about Jesus: he is true man; he is true god. If he was true man he suffered. If he was true god he didn't. There are two ways of thinking about the Buddha: he is the one who sat down and meditated and found his Buddha consciousness; he is the incarnation of Buddha consciousness and he didn't have to meditate at all—he knew it.

The Buddha was born from his mother's side. That means, insofar as his historical message is concerned and his historical character, he was not talking about nature. He was talking about the virgin birth, the nature of the spiritual life. He had experienced the virgin birth himself, you might say, from his mother's side at the level of the heart, not at the level of the pelvic natural birth. No sooner was he born than the deities came down and received him on a golden cloth. Nobody thinks this happened. The dynamic feats of saviors are symbolic of the meaning of the saviors' teaching. It's not like Carl Sandburg's life of Lincoln, where you get documentation of the actual details of the life. It has nothing to do with what happened in life. It has to do with the implications of the life. So the Buddha is born, the gods receive him on a golden cloth, they put him on the ground, and this little child takes seven steps, and his right hand lifts and his left hand points down and he says: "Worlds above, worlds below, there's no one in the world like me!"

He didn't have to go to work to find that out. He knew it when he was born. Daisetz Suzuki, during his first lecture in the United States on Buddhism, mentioned this. He said, "You know, that's very funny thing, baby just born, to say a thing like that! You think he would have waited, waited until he had his illumination under the bo tree and his spiritual birth. But we in the Orient all mixed up. We don't make great distinction between spiritual and material life. Material manifests spiritual." So then he went on in a long talk, pretending to lose all his notes. In Japanese and Chinese paintings, there is a lot of vacant space and you can read something into that. So he left us vacant space by pretending to lose his notes so we could help him find them and feel participation in the lecture. To do too well is not nice.

Finally Suzuki came to this point. "They tell me when baby is born, baby cries. What does baby say, when baby cries? Baby says: 'Worlds above, worlds below, no one in the world like me!' All babies Buddha babies."

The little baby is a Buddha baby. It's a manifestation in innocence of these wonderful energies. So what's the difference between any little mouse and Queen Maya's? Hers knew he was a Buddha baby. The whole thing of Buddha consciousness means getting to know you are it. That takes a lot of work, principally because society keeps telling you you are *not* it.

When this quester, this seeker, this one who is about to become the Buddha, came to the tree in the middle of the universe, the *axis mundi,* which is called the immovable spot, he sat there. That's a psychological condition. You don't have to go to Bodh-Gaya to find the immovable spot. You've got it right here, if you have it. And what is it? It is the spot that is not moved by desire and fear.

So to test him, there came the lord of the world, and his name was desire and fear. As desire he was called Kama, which means lust, desire, delight, pleasure. He tried to move the Buddha by displaying to him his three beautiful daughters. Their names were Desire, Fulfillment, and Regret. Future, present, past. The Buddha had disengaged himself from the biology of this body, and so he wasn't moved. Kama was unhappy about that, and he turned himself into Mara, the Lord of Death, to inspire fear. He threw against the Buddha all the weaponry

of an army of ogres. There was nobody there. This is why we don't see him in the early works; he was not present as a body. He had disengaged himself. And so the weapons were turned into lotuses as they entered his field of nonentity, and he was, as it were, worshiped.

Now comes the hard one for good Christians to appreciate. Kama/Mara was desperate and he turned himself now into Dharma, the Lord of Social Duty. That's supposed to be Christianity. How in heaven's name are you going to find your own track if you are always doing what society tells you your duty is? So it's at this point that Mara, now as Dharma, Duty, says to him, "Young Prince, you are supposed to be on your throne governing a country, don't you read the morning paper? Don't you know what's going on? Things are falling apart. There are picket lines all over the place." What do you do when that call comes? He just dropped his hand and touched the earth. This is: "Don't try to move me with this journalistic appeal. I'm interested in eternity." And he calls the goddess, Mother Universe, to witness to his right to be there. She, in her majesty, with a voice that resounds like thunder on the horizon, says, "This is my beloved son, who through innumerable lifetimes has so given of himself that there is nobody here." And with that, the elephant on which Dharma was riding bowed in worship, the army was dispersed, and the Buddha achieved illumination.

So that symbolizes Akshobhya, not to be moved. This is the first position. You have found it. You are sitting there. You are in the immovable spot and no appeal of the journalistic field of time is going to move you. That's the first step. The second step is, having found the still point, to come back into the field of time.

So we have two Buddhisms: the earlier small-vehicle Buddhism that's going away from the field of time and then, later, the Buddhism that says we are manifestations and we can move in this field of time, but without being moved. This is known as "joyful participation in the sorrows of the world." And you can do that, be what is known as a bodhisattva, one whose "being" (*sattva*) is "illumination" (*bodhi*). With that still point having been found, you can move into the field of movement and not move. That's the important thing.

Heinrich Zimmer, a gifted interpreter of symbolic forms, was lecturing in New York on Buddhism, and he wanted to describe the difference between the little-vehicle Buddhism, Hinayana, and the big-vehicle Buddhism, Mahayana. He used a wonderful image. When the Buddha achieved illumination that night he was so stunned that he sat for seven days in one place without moving. This is being utterly removed from the field of time. Then he got up and walked seven paces back and stood for seven days looking at the place where he had been sitting. This is relating the temporal to the immovable realization. Then for seven days he walked back and forth between the two places, relating and integrating. He then sat down under another tree, and his first thought was, "This cannot be taught." That's the first fact about Buddhism, and what I'm talking about here. This cannot be taught. You know the saying: "You can lead a girl to Vassar, but you can't make her think."

No sooner had he had that thought than the gods Indra and Brahma came down. Just as in Christianity the deity of the older tradition is still present, so in Buddhism the deities of the older tradition are present.

Indra and Brahma said, "Please teach, for the salvation of mankind and the gods and all the world." And the Buddha said, "I will teach. But what I teach is not Buddhism; it is the way to Buddhism." What's called Buddhism is a vehicle to carry you to Buddhist realization, and the word for vehicle is *yāna*, and the vehicle specifically that is referred to is a ferryboat. So Buddhism is called the ferryboat, and it's taking us to a yonder shore, and the yonder shore is the shore beyond pain and pleasure, gain and loss, fear and desire, you and me. It's the transcendence of duality in the realization of the cosmic unity, or transcosmic unity.

Zimmer then said, "Well now, if we want to understand Buddhism and the two Buddhisms—Hinayana and Mahayana, little ferryboat and big ferryboat—let's think about a ferryboat." We are in Manhattan. There's the Hudson River, and beyond the river is New Jersey, the Garden State. We've never been to Jersey, but we've heard about it and we're fed up with Manhattan. We go down to the riverbank and we stand there looking across at Jersey. Jersey for us is simply a mirage before the eyes. We don't know what's over there, but we're longing to be there. We're thinking about it because Manhattan's gotten to be just too much. Well, one fine day, what do you know! From the yonder shore a ferryboat comes across, right to our feet. In the ferryboat is a man, and the man says, "Anyone for Jersey, the Garden State?" You say, "I'm for Jersey." Then he says, "Now, listen. There's a point here, namely, you can't come back. This is a one-way trip. You're giving up your family, your ideals, your money, your future, everything. Are you ready to quit?" You say, "I am

fed up." He says, "Get aboard."

This is the little ferryboat, Hinayana; only those who are ready and willing to quit the whole show can go across. And we read in the texts, "Unless you are as eager for nirvanic release as a man with his hair on fire would be for a pond into which to dive, don't start, it's too difficult." So here we have the idea of great ascetic difficulty and renunciation. This is why it's a little ferryboat. So you get aboard.

The boat starts out and you think, "Mother!" But it's too late, you're in the boat. You learn to love the splash of the water. You learn to speak in a new language—*port* and *starboard* instead of *left* and *right; fore* and *aft* instead of *front* and *back*. You don't know any more about Jersey than you did before you left, but you've come to think of the people in Manhattan as fools. So there you are. There's very little to do, really—lift sails, pull them down again, paddle a little bit, pray. You are a monk or a nun, putting flowers on altars, counting beads, now on this hand, now on that, and so forth and so on. Life's been reduced to something sweet and simple. The last thing you want is to arrive at the other shore and find out there's something else to do. However, after a couple of incarnations (you thought it was going to be a short trip, nothing of the kind, this is a long job), the boat scrapes ashore in Jersey. Ah! This is the exciting moment. We're there. This is what is known as rapture. You step ashore. It's a different world. Finally you think, I wonder what Manhattan looks like from here?

With respect to the passage, the Buddha says: "Suppose a man wishing to get to the yonder shore should build himself a raft, and now having arrived at the yonder shore, with respect for the raft, should pick the raft up and carry it on his shoulders. Would that be an intelligent man?" "Oh no, master," said the monks. So it is with the laws of the order, they have nothing to do with Nirvana. Nirvana transcends all this. The laws of the order are the vehicle that gets you there.

This is the Hinayana, up to now. We're leaving Manhattan and going to Jersey. We're leaving samsara, the vortex of pain, and going to a nirvanic release. You're in New Jersey, you turn around to see Manhattan: you're in the realm of nonduality. You're in the world of transcendence of all pairs of opposites. There's no Manhattan over there. There's no Hudson River between. There's no ferryboat. There's no man in the boat. This is it. That's all it is. You have gone past duality and the realization is: I was there all the time. It's just a transformation of the eyes. Like that saying in the apocryphal Gospel of Thomas, "The kingdom of the father is spread upon the earth and men do not see it." See it! The radiance is all around us here, right now! This is it, and the multiplicity is unity in a wonderful sort of display. So that's the Mahayana. We're there, and yet we're on the ferryboat, and the ferryboat is there. And who's on the ferryboat? There's nobody on the ferryboat. This is the wonderful paradox of Buddhism. The key word is *anātman*. All things are without a self. We're all manifestations of that transcendence. The notion of self is exactly what is separating us from other people. Dissolve that. Don't be afraid, yield. Become the food of others. When that happens, you're in the whole thing. And this is known then as the great delight, mahasukha.

And what then is finally the best austerity, what is the best discipline? The best discipline is: Enjoy your friends, Enjoy your meals. Realize what your play is. Participate in the play, in the play of life. This is known as mahasukha, the great delight. So there comes this final saying, *Bhoga* is yoga. Delight and enjoyment *(bhoga)* a form of yoga. That is the whole theme of T. S. Eliot's *The Cocktail Party*. You've got to give a party? That's your ritual, to realize the presence. It's a wonderful thing. That's the great Buddhism.

An interesting thing is that this development of Mahayana Buddhism took place in northwest India, mostly, in the first two centuries A.D., which were precisely the centuries of the development of Christianity. The idea of the bodhisattva is the one who, out of his realization of transcendence, participates in the world. That's the idea of the Christ, in his love for the world, coming to be crucified—participating in the crucifixion, intentionally, with joy. What's the invitation of Christ? The invitation of Christ is joyful participation in the sorrows of the world, if you read it this way. So there is a wonderful dialogue here when you think of the Christ in the way of the Buddha. These are two folk manifestations of the same elementary idea. The lesson the Buddha tells you is, "You are it." All right. What's the invitation of Christ? Joyful participation, come into this crucifixion with joy, not fear, not desire, and it's a rapture. That's the story there.

Now, many rituals associated with war, in the old days, had to do with getting the warriors into what is known as a "berserk attitude," where you go into the pain of the war with rapture. You are wild participating in this thing. That is a religious approach to war. And so we have the two Buddhisms: the Buddhism of the ascetic effort and the Buddhism of the joyful participation; the little ferryboat, the big ferryboat. "We're there" is big ferryboat stuff. The other one—"You're working hard"—is more little ferryboat. Now some people like to work hard, so the worst thing you can do is say, "Gee, you're having a ball." "No, I'm having a terrible time, and that's the whole sense of my life." Another person might require a different doctrine.

This is the Bodh-Gaya, the actual tree under which the Buddha sat. So we can concretize the whole thing, we can go to Bodh-Gaya. There's a big temple there that depicts the stages of the heavens. The idea is that reincarnation is the counterpart in the Orient of purgatory in the West. When you die, and are so bounded by your ego and its intentions and desires and fears that you can't open to the transcendent revelation of the beatific vision which would annihilate egoism, then you have to be purged (purgatory) of your ego. And this is a kind of postgraduate course that is given to you in a good Christian tradition. In the Oriental tradition, you would be reborn to have another chance. So you keep getting reborn until you are cleansed of ego. But in between incarnations you will go either to a heaven or to a hell, depending on how you behaved. If you responded as well as you could to the disciplines of your

life, you will go to a heaven for which you are ready. If you resisted, you will be sent to a hell where real tough deities will smash you up and make you sorry for yourself.

Now the heaven that you go to will be appropriate to your condition. Nobody is judging you and saying that you've got to go to this heaven or to that hell. Your own psyche has a kind of specific gravity that carries you just to the right heaven. If you are ready for rock and roll, it won't assign you to a chamber music concert. The heaven that you will enjoy will be appropriate to your readiness. The heavens grade up. The lower heavens are those of erotic delights of one kind or another. Next up are those of philosophical contemplation and so forth. Up above it's the transcendence, the meditation on the transcendent, and finally you dissolve. That's the world mountain. Beneath it are the abyssal hells, also graded. Dante's *Divine Comedy* gives us exactly that. The difference between Dante's hell and the hell of Thomas Aquinas is this: Aquinas's hell is just sheer punishment while Dante's hell is appropriate to the way you lived your life. Dante's heaven is also. So the future transcendent is simply a reflection of your present earthly character and being.

The Buddha and Confucius share an important date, 500 B.C. But the Bud-dha sought Nirvana, the stillpoint, while Confucius emphasized social participation. Through social participation, the Tao, the way, the life order, is recognized and participated in and brought into manifestation. Confucius's dates are something like 551 to 478 B.C. It's right on the line of the Buddha's dates, 563 to 483 B.C. Confucius is the key man for the Far East. Behind Confucius is another figure, known as Lao-tzu. Here they are talking to each other. These aren't actually portraits of the men; nobody knows what they looked like. But Lao-tzu means "the old boy," the old sage who identifies himself with a kind of *puer eternus*, with the Tao.

They tell me that in China the two great attitudes are the Confucian and the Taoist. Where society is in form, the Confucian mood prevails, which is participation in the way of the society through the rites of the society. They have nothing to do with sacrifice and ritual in the old sense. They have to do with participation in the social order. When the society goes berserk, then people move toward the Taoist position, which is unification with the universe—the Tao of the universe. The Taoist sage, a typical one you might say, is on the mountaintop. He's let the briars grow in the gate to his hut, he unites with the universe. (Or you can unite with society.) In any case,

in China, and one feels this very strongly, there is a much stronger accent on positive participation in the flow than in India. Even in the "Bhoga is yoga" of the Mahayana in India, you still feel, "Well, we wish we were out of it." But in China there is this marvelous grounding participation.

Lao-tzu represents the Tao in nature; Confucius adapts it to the Tao in society. Remember 500 B.C., the Buddha in India, Confucius in China.

Now we come to the Near East and Darius I, 523–486 B.C. He was the master. What is the idea here? The idea is of the emperor as incarnation, or representative of the king of kings—God as king of kings, and human beings as God's subjects. Here is the idea of man as the servant of God, man as the subject of God, man as the slave of God. This has come down to us.

When I was in school, we recited the catechism "Why did God make you?" "God made me to love him, to serve him, and to honor him in this world and to be happy with him forever in heaven." It has to do with the relationship to God. God did not make me to realize my godhood. That's a totally different thing. We are on the other side of the line. This is the Near Eastern system out of which our biblical heritage comes. Now that is outstanding and different.

In Greece, at the same time, Pythagoras flourished. You'd think you were in India again. One of the most accessible statements of the Pythagorean position is by Ovid in the *Metamorphoses*. He tells of the sage of Samos, who was far from the gods but in his mind at home with them. And what did this sage teach? "All things change, but they are one. The one wax takes many molds." It's the same old doctrine.

So here we have it: in between the Indo-European classical Greek and Indo-European Indian—and beyond that, the Chinese—we have this authoritarian king-of-kings tradition, which has come to us through the Bible. I don't know how it got there, but it's there.

In fifth-century Greece, with Aristotle, something else comes in: rational philosophy and the humanistic tradition—man as man, which is not in the Orient at all—the idea of man as himself the center without bondage to deities. The deities are there as echoes, but they themselves represent powers of man.

If we are to think of the old perennial philosophy as a manifestation to our mental mind of the wisdom of the body, we may think of the Aristotelian approach as addressed to and from the mental. When you are reading Aristotle—whether it's his *Aesthetics* or *The Soul* or whatever—you realize that what he's doing is rendering through

rational terminology references to, and something of the implications of, the older tradition. He's talking about the soul and about transcendence of rationality by means of rational language. What has happened since is that the rational has taken over, and the reference to the transcendence drops out. That's one of the characteristics of our tradition. So in the West we have these two heritages: Aristotle and the Bible. Aristotle's rationality was rational in its reference to something transcendent of rationality, but it has become increasingly strictly rational. In the Bible the stress is on the ethnic rather than the elementary aspect of the message. And these two have given us a commitment to time and space in and for itself, against which the transcendence of the perennial philosophy comes as a threat. A lot of people get the feeling of being threatened by this other thing because it threatens their rational, ethnic, stance.

Now comes the great moment. Aristotle's student is Alexander the Great. In 332 B.C., at the Battle of Arbela, he defeats Darius III. A young, brilliant soldier, whose father was a great military man, Alexander invents military methods that go way beyond what anyone has thought of before. And within fifteen years, he has conquered all of the older systems in the Near East. Persia falls and he rushes through to India. He enters the Punjab around 327 B.C., and it is there that the first encounter of the Western mind and the Oriental guru takes place.

Alexander had a lot of young officers who were students of Aristotle and other philosophers. They had heard that there was a school of Indian philosophers out in the forest, and so, with about ninety-eight interpreters, they go out to talk to this school. What they find is a group of naked old codgers sitting on a burning hot rock. When they propose to talk philosophy, the old yogis say, "Who can talk philosophy with young men wearing military boots and capes? Take your clothes off, sit on a rock for about ninety years, then we can begin to talk."

But one of them was interested. He got up to the jeers of all the others and went off with these chaps and became quite a favorite at Alexander's banquet table. Alexander may have been a little bit tired of Aristotle by that time. The old yogi became really a great favorite and was given presents and gifts. But when the army turned back into Persia, he asked them to build him a great pyre. He climbed up, sat in yoga posture on top of the pyre, and with the elephants of Alexander's army trumpeting and doing sunwise turns around the pyre, he went up in flames. This was Europe's first en-

counter with the philosophy of the East, and it hasn't recovered since.

In India, because of Alexander, there was a ripple effect and the fall of one dynasty after another. We find as late as the first century B.C., in Orissa, at the other end of India, Greek soldiers—Greek mercenaries—guarding temples. And favorites in the harems of north India at that time were the Greek women. So a very strong Greek influence takes hold. And the most important figure to derive from this in India was Ashoka. His dates are the middle of the third century B.C., around 250 B.C. Ashoka was the first emperor to become a Buddhist. It is thought he may have been a Jain before that. He had conquered the north of India and a good deal of the east, but then he became overwhelmed with the realization of the sorrow that he had brought about through his conquests. The Buddhist realization, "All life is sorrowful," overwhelmed him, and he became a Buddhist.

He was the first Buddhist monarch, and he sent missionaries—now this is important—to Ceylon. He sent his own son and daughter to Ceylon to found the mission there. He sent missionaries also—and these are recorded in statements that are engraved in rock and marble—to Macedonia, to Cyprus, and to Egypt. So about 250 B.C. we begin to have Buddhist missionar-

ies in the Near East, and it is at that time that neo-Platonic philosophy begins to arrive. There have been important studies—one by a German named Garba, for example—of parallels between neo-Platonic and Sankhya philosophies. And there's no doubt about it. The influence began coming over, so we begin then to have a synthesis of Eastern and Western thinking.

Now we come to the beginning of Buddhist, and really Hindu, architecture. This is from Ashoka's time at Sanchi. It is called a stupa, and what it represents is a reliquary, a burial mound within which relics are kept. But it is symbolic of the world. It's the cosmic egg. In the stupa, old pre-Buddhist deities are shown paying respect to the Buddha. That's the wonderful thing about Buddhism. Whenever it goes anyplace, it doesn't say, "Cut out your gods." There is a very easy synthesis of religions where Buddhism goes. The characteristic of the Muslim and Christian traditions is to annihilate the gods of the country that they enter. The characteristic of the more gentle Buddhist tradition is that these gods are the local powers of life, which are themselves manifestations of Buddha consciousness. So there they stand in reverence to the revelation of their own Buddhahood.

7

From Id to Ego in the Orient: Kundalini Yoga, Part I

The idea of yoga is already given in the name, *yoga*. It comes from the root *yuj*, which means "to yoke," to connect or join something to something else. What is being yoked is our ego consciousness, the *aham* consciousness, to the source of con-

sciousness. Just as the idea of deity in these perennial traditions greatly differs from our Western idea of deity, so does the idea of consciousness. In speaking of deities in the terms that are proper to these mythologically grounded traditions, I'd say the deity is a personification of the energy. It's a personification of an energy that in-

forms life—all life, your life, the world's life. The nature of the personification will be determined by historical circumstances. The personification is folk; the energy is human. Deities proceed from the energies. They are the messengers and vehicles, so to say, of the energies.

Our idea of deity is that the deity

is a fact, and it's from that fact that the energies proceed. Likewise, with respect to consciousness, our notion is that the brain is the source of consciousness. The traditional idea is that the brain is a function of consciousness. Consciousness is first. The brain is an organ that encapsulates consciousness and focuses it in a certain direction, in the direction of time and space knowledge, which is secondary knowledge. The notion that we are all manifestations of that transcendent consciousness, which goes beyond all our powers to think and to name, is the basic idea of all of this life. In our Western thinking there have been moments when this has come in, against what might be called mainstream philosophy, or the school philosophies.

Long before the Middle Ages, we have Dionysius the Areopagite, a mystical philosopher. His philosophy is picked up in the eighth and ninth centuries in Ireland by John Scotus Erigena, a gnostic philosopher of magnificent concepts. In the High Middle Ages, Meister Eckhart uses the complicated, concretizing language of Christianity, but he blows it apart and you have the recognition of the relationship of the deity to the knower of the deity.

In Renaissance Italy, Cosimo de' Medici invited Marsilio Ficino to translate a text that had been brought from Byzantium by a Byzantine monk. This was the Greek text of the *Corpus hermeticum*, the hermetic philosophy of the first centuries A.D., contemporary with early Christianity but in the pagan terminology. When this appeared, the excitement in the whole world of the arts was enormous. Botticelli's work is full of all of this, and the wonderful flowering of Renaissance art is eloquent of these very ideas that I am talking about. Later you have people like Giordano Bruno, who was burned at the stake in Rome in the year 1600 for saying these things.

Then, in later times, we have Immanuel Kant. There are two kinds of philosophies in the world; there is English philosophy, where nobody really understood what Kant was saying, and there's the philosophy that we find just implicit, for example, in the middle European systems. What Kant recognized, in his *Critique of Pure Reason*, was that all of our knowledge, all of our experience, is conditioned by the organs of experience and the organs of knowledge. *A priori*, primary, antecedent to our experience of anything is our knowledge of time and space. Everything comes to us in a field of time and space. In that wonderful work of his called *The Foundation of Metaphysics*, Kant asked this question: "How is it that we can make determinations for relationships in space here and know that these will work in space there?" And he answers, "It's because the laws of space are right in our own mind." Well, this struck me like dynamite.

During the Apollo flight around the moon, the one that preceded the landing, Ground Control in Houston asked, "Who's navigating now?" The answer that came back, and I heard it with amazement, was "Newton." Now the laws that would work in that space up there, where nobody had ever been before, were known so perfectly that it was possible to bring that little spacecraft back from around the moon and land it within a mile of a little boat in the Pacific Ocean. No matter how far these vehicles go out into space, we've enveloped it. We know it. But when Neil Armstrong's foot came down on the moon, nobody knew how deeply it was going to sink into the moon dust. That is *a posteriori* knowledge. But the framing order of knowledge, through which all of our experiences come, this we already know.

But what is the thing that we're coming to know through time and space? Is it a thing? No. Things are in time and space. You've gone into the transcendent there. So Kant calls this "transcendental aesthetics." After you've seen everything you begin

thinking about it, and the laws of your thinking are what determine what you can think. These are the laws of logic, the categories, and you can't think of anything that doesn't fit in those. So you are enclosed. This is maya—exactly.

It was Schopenhauer who first recognized that the Indian concept of maya and Kant's concept of the forms of sensibility and the categories of logic were equivalent. So in his *World as Will and Idea* he's able to talk about Western thinking in terms of Oriental thinking. The two come right together there. Nietzsche also picked this up, and we have a whole new thrust in Western school philosophy. So these are very important moments in the Western philosophical tradition— these recognitions of the breakthrough of this elementary idea system, the perennial philosophy, into what might be called the school system.

Yoga, then, is a linking of consciousness, this *aham* consciousness, this ego consciousness, to the source of consciousness. The source of consciousness is, of course, transcendent of all our concepts.

When you ask "Is God one or many?" *one* and *many* are concepts. These are the categories of thought. And the word *God* is not supposed to refer to a personality. It's supposed to refer past the personality to that which is really transcendent of thought. The mythic symbols open like that to transcendence.

Jung makes a distinction between the word *symbol* and the word *sign*. This is an arbitrary definition that he uses. A symbol is a mythic symbol which has one leg here and the other in infinity. It points to the transcendent. A sign points to something here. As normally interpreted, God is a sign, not a symbol. The word *God* refers to what is supposed to be a fact. There is a saying I like to quote that came up in the gnostic period, "The problem with Yahweh is that he thinks he's God." That is to say, he says, "I'm it! I'm no symbol." And then, of course, when he's the only one that's it, then everybody else's god is no god at all.

In proper language, concretizing the image, concretizing the symbol, is what we call idolatry, so that our whole religion from this standpoint is an idolatrous system. Perhaps it's because of this unconscious idolatry of our own that we see idolatry in everybody else and smash their idols. That's just a little thought for the day.

The classic book of yoga is called the Yoga Sutra. The word *sūtra* is related to our own *suture*, the thread that a doctor uses to sew you up. So *yoga sutra* means "the thread of yoga." There is a type of book from India called a sutra. There are a lot of sutras,

and they are the sorts of books students buy the night before an examination. In very short concise formulae they summarize the work that you've been doing all year, but you can't really understand the book unless you already know the subject.

Now the opening aphorism of the Yoga Sutra, which is attributed to a legendary sage named Patanjali, is the classic definition of yoga: "Yoga is the intentional stopping of the spontaneous activity of the mind stuff."

There are two aspects to the physiology of the mind. One is the nerves, the gray matter, and the other is the energy that lives in the nerves. The energy is what communicates the messages. The gross matter is called, in Sanskrit, *sthūla*. The subtle matter, the energy inside, the activating principle, is called *sukshma* ("subtle").

This subtle matter within the brain takes the forms of what impacts the senses. We see things as though they are in our heads because the subtle matter has taken their forms. And we hear things for the same reason, and so forth, and so on. Move your eyes quickly, and you'll see how quickly the subtle matter changes. The problem is that it continues to change even when you want it to stand still. Suppose you wanted to hold in your mind one thought, or one image, something you think you'd like to hold there. You will find that within four or five seconds you are having associated thoughts. The mind is moving.

The goal of this yoga is to make the mind stand still. Why should you want to do that? We're coming to a basic idea in this perennial philosophy —namely, that everything is experienced through the mind. This is maya. The mind is in an active state. The image is given of a pond rippled by a wind. The rippling pond with its waves reflects images that are broken. They come and go, come and go, come and go. In the Book of Genesis, the wind, the breath, the spirit of God blew over the waters. That's the creation of the world. You start this excitement going.

Now comes the point. What we do is identify ourselves with one of those broken images, one of those broken reflections on the surface of the pond. Here I come: There I go. That links us to the temporal flow, time and space —maya. Make the pond stand still, one image. What was broken and reflected is now seen in its still perfection, and that's your true being. But that's everybody else's true being also. This is the goal of yoga, to find that reality of consciousness which is of you and of everybody else.

Schopenhauer's *World as Will and Idea* is full of this. The book is a symphony of rapture dealing with this matter. He uses an image that I like to bring up in relation to this in his *Foundations of Morality*. He asks, "How is it that a human being can so participate in the danger and peril of another that, forgetting his own self-protection, he moves spontaneously to that person's rescue?" How is it that what we take to be the first law of nature, preserving this separate entity, this ego, is suddenly dissolved; and, as though one were that other, one acts spontaneously in the interests of that other— even at the risk of one's own life. One acts spontaneously to save a little child that's about to be run over. Schopenhauer answers by saying, "This is a metaphysical realization that has broken through which is usually not there." It's the realization of the universal consciousness of which we are all manifestations. So in that sense you and that other are one.

The experience of separateness is only a secondary experience within the *a priori* frame of time and space which is the separating principle, what Nietzsche calls the *principium individuationis*, the individuating principle of time and space. If it weren't for time and space we would not be separate here. So this is our secondary experience. You have to have this experience in order to live in the world, but every now and then there's a breakthrough to the other realization.

So the function of yoga is to release us from the time–space commitment, introduce us to the transcendent. Then comes the problem of bringing us back so that we can operate in both knowledges.

The dates for the sutras are usually given as sometime between 200 B.C. and A.D. 200. In those four hundred years this thing took its shape. The yoga that I want to discuss is a specific late form of yoga that developed in the fourth and fifth centuries. It's known as Kundalini yoga, and it affected all of the Eastern religious structures. It appears in Buddhism, in Jainism, in Hinduism, almost simultaneously. So I'm going to use both Buddhist and Hindu images to illustrate it.

Kundalini comes from the word *kundalin,* which means "coiled up." The reference is to the spiritual energy that is coiled up, as it were, at the base of the spine, the base of the body. When it is in that condition, coiled up down there, there's not much spiritual life. The spiritually energized organs are in the lower pelvic area. The goal of the yoga is to wake that coiled-up energy and bring it up the spine. It's pictured as a serpent, a little female serpent, because, again, the energy is female. Action is also female, *shakti.* It's a little female serpent called the kundalini, a coiled-up female serpent, pictured

about as thick as the hair of a boar, white, and coiled three and a half times around a symbolic *lingam,* a symbolic male organ which is there at the base of the body also. This is all "subtle" substance. You won't find it on the operating table. It is coiled three and a half times, with the head of the serpent over what is called the Brahma door of the *lingam* so that the energies do not come up. The goal of the yoga is to wake that serpent and bring her up the spine. On the way up she passes seven centers. The center at the base is called *mūlādhāra,* the root base; the center at the crown of the head is called *sahasrāra,* the thousand-petaled lotus; and in between are five other centers. As that serpent power enters the field of those sequential centers, the whole psychology of the individual is transformed.

I'm going to use this as a means to link into our Western philosophies and see where each of them stands in relation to this. It's a very, very recondite and long-seasoned philosophical concept, as Jung says when he discusses the *Tibetan Book of the Dead:* "These people are so far ahead of us that we've got only up to the third cakra." Jung himself, I would say, had got to the fourth. "But," he says, "we've got to move into this slowly, and don't have the notion that we understand all these things, because we have not had the experience systems yet that interprets them.''

So with that little introduction, we start, and we start by meditating. This is said to be a comfortable posture. We are to sit with the spine perfectly erect.

Since the human body and the cosmic body are equivalent, our spine is comparable to the world axis. So we have reached the world axis, the central point, the immovable spot, and we are now in meditation.

You begin by breath control, breath-

ing to certain paces, and the breath is very curious. You breathe in through one nostril, hold, breathe out through the other nostril, hold, in through the second, hold, out through the first, and so forth and so on. The notion is that emotion and feeling and state of the mind are related to breath. When you are at rest, the breathing is in a nice, even order. When you are stirred with shock the breathing changes. With passion the breathing changes. Change the breathing and you change the state. What we are trying to do is smooth the waters of the rippled pond by slow breathing. The length of the breath of one of these priests is terrific.

The practiced yogi has a great chestful of breathing possibilities.

So we're going to calm the waters. And when the waters are calm, that image of images appears, is known to us. Now comes a point. Here is the gross outer body, and held in the hands is a representation of the subtle body. Do not identify the gross body with the subtle body. If you do that, you are crazy, and you think you are it. So we must disengage. This image represents the totality of the energies of life pouring into the field of time and space; it is what we call God. God is a personification of the energies, and that's it. But these energies show

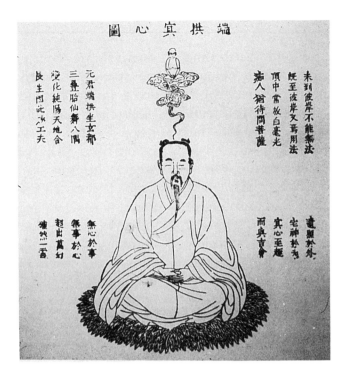

themselves in the world in many aspects. Each organ of the body has its own impulse to action, and the whole problem for our psychology is the conflict of those impulse systems. Each of the organs of nature and of the body has its own inflection of this form.

In the East there are five elements. In the West there are four, but then there are love and hate which pull them together and separate them, which represent the fifth. Now here the fifth is space, *ākāsha*, or as they usually translate it, ether. And then there come air, fire, water, and earth. So this system is a pantheon. There is

a Buddha associated with each of the five, a named Buddha. There's the Buddha of the Center and the Buddhas of the East, the West, the South, and the North.

This whole theme of east, south, west, and north associated with the solar course is a common feature in mythologies everywhere. The sun rises, the new day. The sun at noon is in the south, so the south represents the height, the culmination moment of consciousness in the field of time. In the west, it sinks into transcendence again, and we speak about "going west" when one dies. In the north it is, as it were, under the earth, and that's the area from which demons come, disease comes, dangers come, and tyrannical force comes. In American Indian mythologies, the little heroes who are going to save their mother from the monsters are warned by her not to go north, that's where danger is. They can go east, south, or west. So the boys go north. The only way to get past the rules of the society is to go north, to break the rules. You find something that the society knows nothing about and you bring it back, and that serves as a saving, amplifying, force. So in this eleventh-century Tibetan figure, we have a central Buddha and four more representing east, south, west, and north. The Buddha himself sits at the immovable point—Bodh-Gaya, the Bo tree, the tree of illumination, the Bodhi tree, the tree of awakening.

The word *Buddha* means "the one who has waked up, whose eyes have opened." We carry the eye in our pocket all the time. It is on the back of the dollar bill, at the top of the pyramid, where the sides, the pairs of opposites, come together. There the eye of knowledge opens. But in the field of action you are down on the side. You are on this side and the other guy is on the other side, and so you have action. But this eye is the middle eye, the eye of the referee in the tennis match. It

doesn't care which side wins. You can't have a match unless there is some serious intention to knock the other chap out. So time asks for violence. But this eye asks for the recognition behind the violence, of peace, where the lion lies down with the lamb. This doesn't mean the lion isn't going to eat the lamb. Of course he is going to eat the lamb. But it means nothing is happening when that happens. That's just a temporal thing, and you must realize the peace that lies behind that act. So we have the Buddha under the tree. His eyes have opened as a result of the influence of these other Buddhas. These are meditation Buddhas, Dhyani Buddhas. They are not historical Buddhas; they are subtle matter. It's through their influence that he comes to this knowledge. Ignorance is represented by a pig and is pierced by a lance. With the opening of the eye ignorance is wiped out.

These are the subtle nerves, each one with a name. The word up here is *prānāyāma*, which means breath control. You breathe in and imagine the breath is filling all of these nerves, activating all the senses, all the organs of consciousness. We're going to be more and more conscious. That's the whole point. Demons or monsters are what inhibit consciousness. Many of the demons are our professors and teachers. They set up rules for how we should

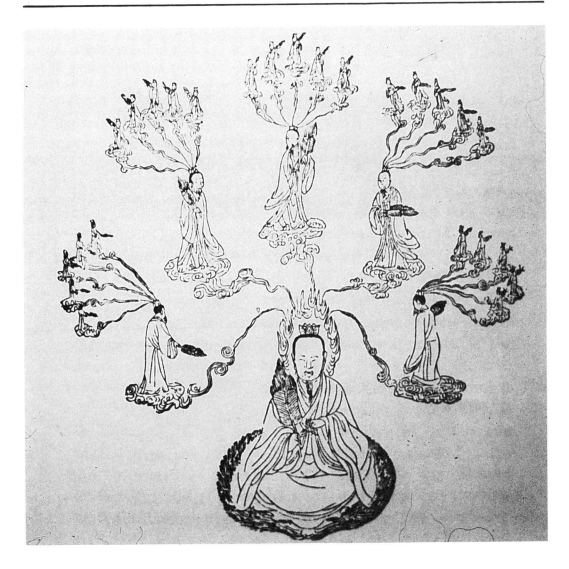

think, and they are not always helpful.

So of this multitude of nerves there are three that are the most important. Here they are, and here are the seven centers. We have a central spine nerve, running up the center of the spine, called *sushumnā*. And on each side is a side nerve. The one that is here rendered gray is called *idā* and refers to lunar consciousness. This is the most important clue to the whole thing —lunar consciousness, consciousness that dies, as the moon does, and is resurrected. The serpent casts away its skin to be born again. So it represents the power of life, energy, and consciousness to throw off death. But it is in the field of death. It is consciousness in the field of death, throwing off death and putting on new bodies— reincarnation or the sequence of the generations. Every time a new generation is begotten, the death of this generation is thrown off and life has moved on.

This throwing off of these bodies and putting on new is symbolic of life energy and consciousness engaged in the field of time, the field of death and birth. The moon sheds its shadow to be born again. The serpent sheds its skin to be born again. They are symbolic of this power.

The other nerve is called *pingalā* and represents solar consciousness. The sun does not die. When it sets it takes

life with it. It does not carry death in itself. This is consciousness disengaged from the field of time.

There are those who begin to feel so very spiritual. You run into them in ashrams. They walk a little above the ground. For them, life is vulgar. I'll never forget my experience the first time I was in an ashram, years and years ago. It was a beautiful place with deer grazing on the lawns and girls in saris on bridges looking down at the goldfish swimming in the pools. It was simply ravishing. Then some vulgarian came into the group. We thought, "How can we tolerate this gross body?" So when you think of your spiritual life as relieving you of the physical, you are going up this track. You are going to have a great disappointment somewhere along the line because your body is still there. This is known as manic-depressive experience. You've identified yourself with the subtle body, but you're still gross. You're trying to become immortal while you are still on earth.

Jesus rejected the devil when the devil said, "Look, young man, you look hungry. Why don't you turn the stones into bread?" Jesus said, "One lives not by bread alone, but by every word out of the mouth of God." Then the devil says, "I'll take you up onto a mountaintop and show you the kingdoms of the world. All you have to do

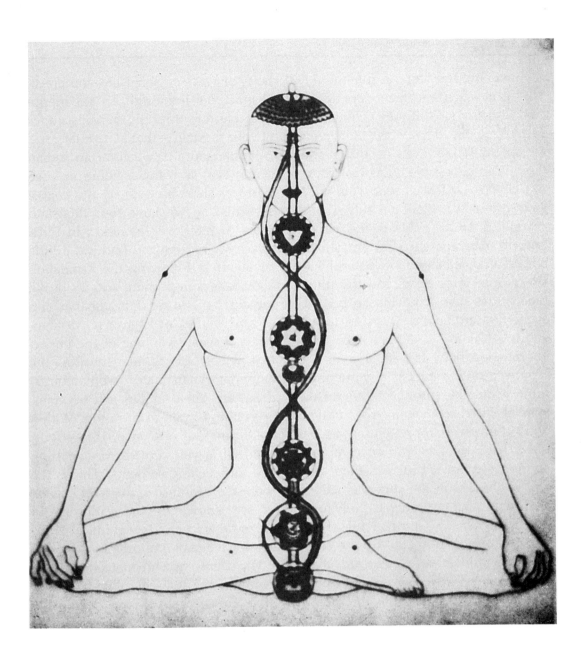

is bow to me and you can rule these." This is how to become a politician. And Jesus says, "Get thee behind me, Satan." So the devil says, "Oh, you are so, so subtle. Let's go up on the top of Herod's temple. Now cast yourself down, God will bear you up." And Jesus said, "No. I am still alive. I am still a body." This is the virtue known as temperance. "I am still a body. Get thee behind me, Satan." He rejects him three times and the third time is this one of having surpassed economics and politics. "You are just a spirit." "Not so." So Jesus is recognizing the gross body as well.

Now people who don't know anything about the spiritual reference of symbols interpret them in gross matter and get involved in pretty gross activities. That is to say, if you interpret the spiritual symbol as concrete, then you get involved with the concrete action associated with the concrete body and you have lost the spiritual message. You can't bring kundalini up the center until you have recognized that these are simply two aspects of the one consciousness. The light of the moon is the reflection of the light of the sun. The light of your body, the consciousness of your body, is immortal, eternal consciousness in you. Consciousness first, then you. You represent the specification of the consciousness in time and place. Through the specifica-

tions of your personal life you are to abstract the immortal. To experience your eternity through the vicissitudes of your mortality, that's the total goal.

From 2000 B.C. we have an Indian stamp seal showing a figure in yoga posture. There are two *idā* and *pingalā* serpents. So we have four thousand years of interior exploration in India which we're going to find out a little bit about in following the Kundalini. Now, this is important, and it's of the same date, 2000 B.C. It is a libation cup of King Gudea of Lagash in Mesopotomia. Lagash was one of the important cities of Sumer during the Sumerian renaissance. Two lion birds, these are later known as cherubim, open the portals of a shrine. Within the shrine are one, two, three, four, five, six, seven centers formed from two interlocking serpents. This is the earliest appearance in the world, as far as we know, of the caduceus of Hermes/Mercury—the guide of souls to knowledge of immortal life.

The cherubim who guard the gate of Paradise, the two cherubim that God placed at the gate to keep man away from the tree of immortal life, are now opening the portal. So you can go in, and there is the tree of life, under which the Buddha sat. And where is that tree? It's right in every one of us. So you don't have to go to Bodh-Gaya. However, if you are interpreting this

142

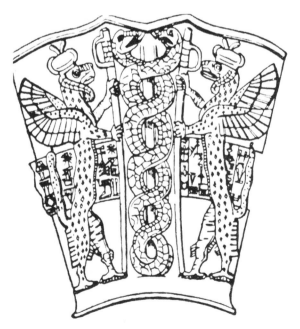

whole thing purely materially, not spiritually, you will go to Bohh-Gaya.

So now we start up the line. These centers are called in Sanskrit *padmas* (lotuses) or *cakras* (wheels). The *c* is transliterated from Sanskrit and pronounced as though it were *ch*. The first center, at the base of the body between the rectum and the sex organs—at the very root of the body—is called the *mūlādhāra* (root base). The yoga posture that we saw before is the *mūla-bandhāsana*, the binding posture, binding the mula. At this level the psyche is practically inert. It is just hanging on to life, and my mental image for this is dragons, which, as we know from biology, guard things in caves. The customs of the dragon have been studied for many millennia. They guard things in caves—beautiful virgins, symbols of Cakra 2, the *cakra* of sexuality; and heaps of gold, Cakra 3, possession and winning. They don't know what to do with either, but they simply guard. This is the condition of the whole psyche when the energy is bound up in the *mūlādhāra*, no zeal for life, no positive action, only reaction.

The psychology appropriate to this dull condition is that of behaviorism. You don't have an active psyche, only a reactive one. Nietzsche calls this position that of groveling before sheer fact. Actually, there's no such thing as sheer fact; it's the object for a subject.

The attitude of the mind beholding the object is what changes the character and meaning of the fact. People who hang on like this we call creeps. They are exactly, you might say, the incarnation of the character of Cakra 1. Art on this level is simply sentimental naturalism. It has no breakthrough to the radiance.

Here is a representation of Cakra 1. The rectangle is of the element earth, the grossest of the elements. In the center is a red triangle, the *yoni*. This is the womb, or the sex organ, of mother cosmos. We are within her womb. She is time–space, including *a priori* forms of sensibility and of the categories of knowledge. It is within that womb that we are.

The *lingam* here, the male organ, represents the energy that breaks into that womb. Now this is interesting and important: the *lingam* represents the energy coming from the transcendent, coming into the womb, but the *lingam* is not antecedent to the womb, because there are no things; there are no pairs of opposites until you get within the womb. So this is a manner of symbolization that's proper to already being in time and space. There is no pair of opposites in the transcendent. It is neither male nor female. When we talk about *brahman* being the still energy and *maya* the active energy, we are talking in dualistic terms

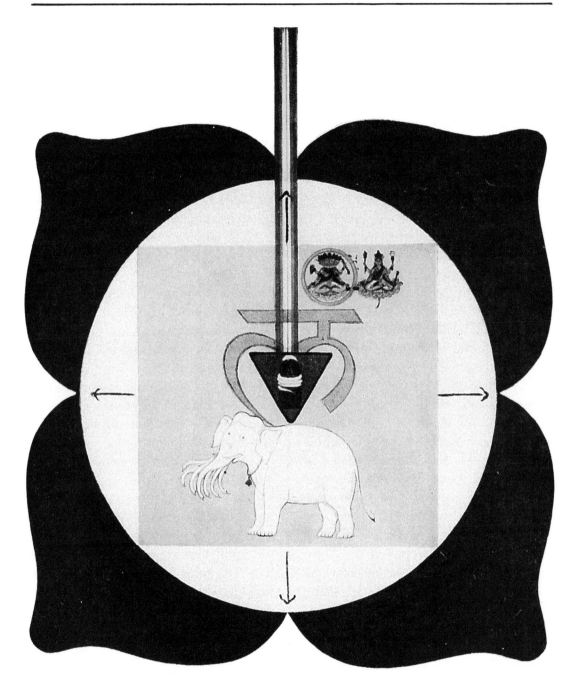

again. The transcendent is transcendent. It transcends all thinking. And so we can't think about it. As Heinrich Zimmer used to say, "The best things can't be said." This is why. "The second best are misunderstood." That's because the second best are using the objects of time and space to refer to transcendence. And so they are always misunderstood by being interpreted in terms of time and space. The third best is conversation. We're trying to use the second best now in order to talk about the first.

So this is the symbol of the generating mystery of the universe. The central form here is the Sanskrit letter *lam;* when the yogi pronounces it, he's activating the energy of this center.

In certain myths, elephants originally could fly and now are bound to the earth. The elephant here is bound to the earth, supporting the whole Kundalini. He has seven trunks and his name is Airavata. He is the cloud on which the god Indra rides. He is the Vedic counterpart of the classical Zeus, king of the gods. Now when Brahma the Creator opened the world egg out of which the whole universe came—we're talking mythologically; the Hindus don't think there was an egg that the god opened—out came nine elephants. One of them was Airavata. The other eight were in four pairs, and they went off to the four

directions and supported the upper shell. So, the elephants are the caryatids of the universe. It's nice to go to a temple, knowing this thing about elephants, and see the elephants holding up the universe. They are clouds that have been condemned to this job. So when you see elephants walking along in the street all clothed and caparisoned, with howdahs on top, remember they're symbolic. You are in the presence of a meditation.

There's a nice story about elephants. A student had just learned from his guru that he was divine. He was what God is. "I am God. Shivo'ham, I am Siva." Deeply meditating on this and wonderfully impressed by himself as God he goes out for a stroll down the street. As he's walking, here comes an elephant his way with a howdah with people up on top. The mahout, the elephant driver seated on the elephant's head, says, "Get out of the way, you fool." The student thinks, "I am God, and the elephant is God. Should God get out of the way of God?" So that's the situation when the elephant comes upon him and simply wraps his trunk around him and tosses him off to the side. He's completely disheveled and psychologically greatly shocked. He goes back to his guru in this terrible shape. The guru sees him coming and says, "So what happened to you?" "Well," the student says, "an elephant

146

threw me off the road. They were shouting for me to get out of the way, but I was in your meditation, what you told me, and I thought, I'm God and the elephant's God, should God get out of the way of God?" "Well," says the guru, "why didn't you listen to voice of God shouting at you to get out of the way?" That's the identification of the gross body with the subtle.

Well, this is known as Srī Yantra. You've seen it, I'm sure, frequently. A *yantra* is a machine. It's from the verbal root *yan*, to help us do something. A

147

yantra is a machine to help us meditate, a support for meditation. What you see in the very center is the triangle that we've just seen. Instead of having the *lingam* represented here, we're seeing it from above. This is called the *bindu,* the drop, the impact of the eternal energy in and on the field of time. When the field of time is struck, it breaks into pairs of opposites. So we always have pairs of opposites.

I was in Japan and was taken to Nagasaki, where the second atom bomb was dropped. I was with a group of Japanese, and I must say I felt mortified, being an American, and responsible—remotely—for this horrific act. The extent of devastation was still evident. They have an enormous image just pointing up, exactly to the place from which the bomb came. My Japanese friends felt no malice, no sense of my being to blame. We had been enemies, pairs of opposites, two aspects of the same thing—beautiful. If you begin to think of things that way, it's the process of Brahman.

There is a little meditation for meals of the Ramakrishna monks. It's right out of the *Bhagavad-Gita.* Brahman is the sacrifice, what is being killed. Brahman is the ladle of the sacrifice, the instrument through which the sacrifice takes place. Brahman is the fire of the sacrifice, that fire which then consumes the sacrifice. He who sees the operation of the Brahman in all things is on the way to realizing himself as a Brahman. So, the most horrible thing that can happen to you, or to your friends, is of Brahman. To see it, then, in the way of a sacrifice and the mystery of the process disengages you from the values of time and space and links you to this other thing: you yourself are simply a bubble, a wave on the rippling surface.

A series of red petals represents the subtle body, a blue, the gross. And in medieval symbology we have the same colors. Mary, who represents the earthly mother, is always blue; and Christ, in her womb or born, is red. This is the blood of the savior, the subtle mystery. This is the carrier of it all. In your meditation you may think of these triangles as proceeding from the center; that's meditating on creation. You can also see them as going back to the center; that's a meditation on disillusion, or *prayala.* The universe comes and goes. Brahma opens his eyes and closes his eyes, and opens his eyes and closes his eyes. And so all the anxiety about the atom bomb? Meditate on disillusion, that's all. The whole world—not you alone—the whole world comes and goes and comes and goes. It's in the process. This doesn't mean that you mustn't go to work to stop atom bombs. This has to do with relationship to the whole mystery in terms of its metaphysics and with your relationship to the mystery of being. So we can meditate now on disillusion.

Christianity was born out of a meditation on disillusion. In the first centuries B.C. and A.D., the whole Jewish race was excited about the end of the world. The Dead Sea Scrolls tell us all about this. It was going to come. Christianity was born out of this. And then every thousand years the Christians think the world is going to end again. In the year 1000 there were people in France who gave their property to the church, to gain merit just before the end of the world. Some of their descendants are still in the courts, I understand, trying to get the land back. Now, of course, we're coming to the year 2000, so it's time to give it back again. People are meditating on the atom bomb and so forth, so this is a regular cycle in our culture—every thousand years, we have disillusion meditations.

8

From Psychology to Spirituality: Kundalini Yoga, Part II

I was awakened recently by the ringing of the Angelus, which rings nine times and then nine times again. What it is talking about when it rings is the conception of the Christ Child—the pouring of eternal energy into the field of time. That's what the

Angelus is. That's what the 108 names of the goddess is. It's all one story.

When I was in Kashmir, I came upon a ruined temple and in the middle of it there was a *yoni*, the symbol of the female organ. In a temple devoted to the goddess, this is the altar. I later went into one such temple with some Indian friends. We brought of-ferings of fruit and such, and the priest took some of the red powder that women wear on their foreheads and sprinkled it into the *yoni*, reciting the 108 names of the goddess. And 108 times 4 is 432, the number of years in the cycle of time. The goddess is the cycle of time. She is time. She is the womb.

The *lingam* is the male energy of the god. So these are the two symbols of the ultimate energies, the male and female energies, both of which come into separation in the field of time, and neither of which exists transcendent of time. But that which breaks them into the field of time is the female power. So the goddess in this mythology is the high power. In this figure from China, there are one, two, three-and-a-half turns of the serpent power.

That's exactly the kundalini. The figure is in bronze, from the period of the contending states, which puts it around the fifth century B.C., the time of Confucius. This is earlier than any indication of the kundalini in the symbolism of India. A similar serpent is pictured in a basket, the sacred object of the goddess Isis, from Rome, about A.D. 50, the period of Caligula. Again, the serpent is related to the moon: the serpent sheds its skin, the moon sheds its shadow. So you can see that what I'm talking about covers the whole of Eurasia, all the way from Rome to China. But it's only in India that it was brought to full expression and elucidation through the experiences and analyses of these yogic masters.

Let's look back at the representation of Cakra 1. In the upper-right corner is the Hindu God of creation, Brahma, who sits on the lotus that grows from Vishnu's navel. There is his consort Sarasvatī. Here is a beautiful representation from Aihole, from about the fifth century, of Brahma the Creator. He's not really the creator because he's

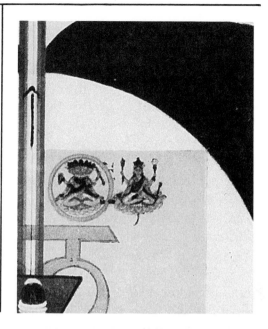

sitting on a lotus. That is to say, the world has already come into being. But what he represents, in these four faces, is the throwing of the light of consciousness out over the field of being, which the lotus represents. Now the lotus is female. This is the goddess herself.

With respect to worship, Brahma holds the ladle of public worship—sacrifice—and the rosary of private meditation. Those are the two ways of approaching the god. What you get from the god is the knowledge of immortality—the elixir of the knowledge of immortality is in the jar. And you receive boons from the god of harmonious life.

At his right knee is a gander, the wild goose, which is at home on the land, in the water, and in the high air. Consequently he is symbolic of the spirit of the lord of the three worlds and informs all of the worlds. The word for gander in Sanskrit is *hamsa*. When you breathe in you hear *ham*, when you breathe out you hear *sa*. Your very breath is telling you all the time you are that hamsa. When you hear it not as *ham-sa*, but as *sa-ham*, it means, "I am that." This is meditation on the breath. Every breath is telling you that what you really are is this spirit that informs the universe. Roundabout are the Rhishis, the

saints, in rapture at the very knowledge of the being of Brahma.

A favorite of mine depicts the bird of the spirit of the breath holding the nine elephants—the nine elephants that support the world. They represent the gross power, and the subtle power supports them. So we've dealt with *mūlādhāra*.

We move up now to Cakra 2, *svādhisthāna*, which means "her favorite resort," her favorite standing place. This is the sex organs. At this cakra the psychology is transformed. It is no longer behaviorism but, rather, the psychology of Dr. Freud. Everything is exciting. Sex is the aim of life. Everything is coming up roses. The birds are singing. The bells are ringing for me and my gal.

The frustrations of sex are also to be recognized here. If the frustrations are continuous, then one turns one's mind to something else, and civilization comes into being. This is what is known as sublimation.

Here is a representation of Cakra 2, and we can see the symbology of the world associated with the psychology of this cakra. In the inner field is a crescent moon. The moon is governor of the tides of life. The whole sex thing is the tide of life; when the moon is full, people are lunatics for sex. The dogs bark, the coyotes howl, and I'm told

that the crabs come out and dance on the beach. Within the crescent is a *makara*, the symbolic animal of the Ganges, the goddess Ganga. The pouring of the waters of the Ganges is this energy, the erotic source of life and of excitement and of being in the world. But Ganga is not the only source. In the Vedic pantheon the god Varuna represents the rhythm of the rolling heavens. In the night sky you can see it moving, and that rhythm is the rhythm of the universe and is of Varuna. The Hindu deity of this cakra is Vishnu, who is associated with the erotic. We see him here, wearing a yellow garment, and he is essentially in an erotic mood.

The incarnation of Vishnu in this aspect that is the favorite in India is Krishna. He who fell in love with Radha, a little married woman. We're breaking past ethics here. This is the love of God for the world, eternity in love with the forms of time. God falls utterly in love with Radha.

There's a beautiful, very voluptuous, poem about this called the *Gita-Govinda* ("The Song of the Cowherd"), composed by a young Brahmin who was in love with the daughter of his guru and saw himself as Krishna and her as Radha. He writes of his love as Krishna informing him, Krishna's love animating his own love.

It is a long, rich, very human and yet divine work. The date for this poem is the twelfth century, about 1170 to 1180, the dates for the Tristan romance in Europe. The whole theme of this "rule-breaking erotics," which underlies the courtly love tradition, belongs to exactly the same century in India. In Japan you have Lady Murasaki's *Genji*, which is about a century earlier and again in the erotic mood. It is through sheer Cakra 2 experience that one can come to divine realization. This is the Vaishnava tradition—the tradition associated with Vishnu—which is of this erotic mode, the way of love. Christ also is love. His love brings him to death on the cross. He is a kind of Vaishnavite incarnation. There are many such parallels between Christianity and Vaishnavism.

There are five orders of love. The earliest and lowest and simplest, for people who are principally interested in something else, is that of master and servant, the servant for the master. "O Lord, you are the master, I the servant. Give me rules to live by and I will live by them. I will do your will." This is for people who are engaged in the activities of life without much time for religious thought. That's about the level on which they worship. You get a heavy dose of this rule-giving principle in the Old Testament with the

Book of Laws, and so forth—rules, rules, rules by which God subjugates you.

The second order of love is that of friend for friend. With the friend you are thinking of him more. This is the order in India of the Pandavas, the boys of the *Mahabharata* and Krishna. It is the order in the Christian tradition of the apostles of Christ. They are close in, they can ask questions, they are thinking of him more, and they come to realizations.

The third order of love is that of parent for child, where the deity is the child. This is the order of the Christmas crib. It's the order of the love in the Hindu tradition for the little naughty boy Krishna, the butter thief,

and so forth. This represents the birth of the spiritual life in your heart. It is just born, it's a tender child. It must be fostered. Now where do you find it? A woman came to Ramakrishna and said, "I find that I do not love God. The concept does not move me." Ramakrishna asked her, "Is there nothing in the world that you do love?" And she said, "Yes, I love my little nephew." He said, "There he is."

There's recognition of the divine in the activities of life. This is good Hinduism, it's good Tantra, it's good Buddhism. Going to temple is quite secondary. Our religious life is here and now. This is the idea that Eliot was trying to incorporate in *The Cocktail Party*, that is, the ritual, the relationship; for it's through relationship —this is the Confucian idea, too, of relationship, person to person—that the Tao is realized.

Then we come to the fourth order of love, marriage, spouse for spouse. The Hindus make much more of the woman's relationship to the husband than of his relationship to her. But the principle is: In the life of marriage and the life together of two people, this is the ritual field. You say, "I do not love God." But there she is, your wife.

The highest order of love is where there is nothing but love—mad, engaged, illicit, careless of the rules of the world, a breakthrough into the transcendent. This is the comparable experience to that of saving somebody at the risk of your own life. Passion, impulse has taken over to such extent that the world has dropped off. This is the idea of courtly love. And believe me, this was a risk in those days, because the punishment for adultery was death.

We've seen these Apsaras, the heavenly dancers riding on the thighs and legs of the heavenly musicians, soaring in rapturous love. We have examples of this on our roads all over the country. The motorcycle couples, cruising along, are perfect incarnations of these Apsaras.

So we come to Cakra 3, *manipūra*, at the level of the navel. *Manipūra* means "City of the Shining Jewel." Here the energy is aggressive: to conquer, to

consume, to turn everything into one-self. We have an Adlerian psychology at this point, a total transformation. One of the problems in the early Freud camp was already recognized here. For Freud, sex was the prime energy; for Adler, it was the will to power. For some people it is one, for some the other. Jung comes in as these two are fighting this thing out and says, "Yes, there are people running this way; there are also people running that way. All of us have both. One is recessive and the other dominant in any given case." So he had this psychology of the duality in what he called *enantiodromia;* you tip over and your sex drive suddenly gives way to a violence drive. Or your winning drive suddenly gives way to sex. They are in opposition to each other in our lives.

So Cakra 3 is a primarily power-dominated cakra, and the Sanskrit here is very important. This is the one from which most of the energies have to be generated. Look at this ominous lotus. The petals are described as having the color of lightning-laden thunderclouds. In the center is the womb, the *yoni*—fire, energy. The swastika motif means movement, energy, violence. The syllable is *ram,* and the animal is a ram. He represents the vehicle of the god of fire, Agni, the fire of the womb, the fire of the sun, the fire of the sacrificial altar. These are all the same fire. They are the transforming fire. The womb is the transforming medium, transforming past into future. The gods here are Shiva, in his violent aspect, and his consort, Lakini, her jaws and breasts smeared with the blood and fat of sacrifices.

Now we get to the deep stuff. Kali is in her Durga aspect. But she is as black time, Kali. *Kali* means "black"; *kali* means "time." That's her name. She is black time out of which all things come, back into which they go—the void, the transcendent, the mother and tomb of all things. "Don't be afraid. Nothing's happening, just a ripple on the surface." Her prime altar is the battlefield, sacrifice. This is the yoga of war. The individual gives himself up to the Lord Death and is not in protection of himself but is moved by the tides of history.

People living on the levels of Cakras 1, 2, or 3 are living on animal levels. Animals, too, cling to life. Animals, too, beget their future. Animals, too, fight to win. So people on these levels have to be controlled by social law, *dharma*. Just think of what our popular religions are concerned with—prayers for health, wealth, progeny, and victory. That is asking the gods to serve your animal nature. This is popular religion. It doesn't matter what the god's

name is. I'll never forget being in Mexico City at the church of the Virgin of Guadalupe. There were swarms of people; and the women, holding their little babies, had traveled on their knees from blocks away to thank the Virgin for their healthy infants. The last time I had seen anything quite like that was at Puri, at the Temple of the Juggernaut. It was the same kind of popular religiosity. And I thought, What is it the popular world wants?

It's health, wealth, and progeny, and it doesn't matter what the god's name is. So that's the one religion, the one popular religion all over the world, no matter what the name of the god is. The job of the priests, those in charge of the historical temple, is to get the name of their god linked up with this thing, and the money pours in like crazy.

Think of the first temptations of the Buddha: the temptation of lust, Cakra

2; temptation of fear, Cakra 3; and the temptation of duty, *dharma.* He had gone past this. We're not in the field of authentic religious life, in the field of the spiritual birth, until we come up to Cakra 4. This is at the level of the heart—the Sacred Heart of Jesus. Jesus, as Leopold Bloom says in *Ulysses,* "with his heart on his sleeve."

Cakra 4 is *anahata,* which means "not hit." *Anā* is "not." *Hata* is "hit." What this refers to is the sound that is not made by any two things striking together. The sound of my voice, any sound you hear, is made by two things striking together. The voice is air striking the vocal cords. What is the sound that is not made by any two things striking together? It is *om.* It is the sound of the energy of the universe of which all things are manifestations. The energy is what underlies all the forms—$E = MC^2$—and the sound of that energy is said to be *om.*

Now *om* can be written in Roman letters either as *o-m* or *a-u-m; o* in Sanskrit is analyzed into *a* and *u.* It is the four-element syllable: *a, oo, mm,* and the silence out of which *om* comes and back into which it goes. The Indians will always recognize that ground in silence, in the infinite, in transcendent, in the void. *Om,* pronounced, starts in the back of the mouth, *a* then fills the mouth cavity, *ooo,* then closes the lips, *mmm.* When properly pronounced, you have made all the noises, and so all words are simply fragments of *om.* Just as all the images of the broken forms of the world are fragments of the form of forms, so all words are fragments of om. *Om* is the sound of the radiance of God.

Om is discussed in a very interesting two-page Upanishad, *Māndūkya,* in terms of its four elements, the four stages. *A* is associated with waking consciousness, the gross bodies of the forms in which we dwell, and of which we are one. Here, I am not you, you are not I, and a duality prevails, an Aristotelian logic. *A* is not Not-*A.* Aristotle's logic is the logic of waking consciousness carried right through, and he's not letting anything else break in there. Gross bodies are not self-luminous. They have to be illuminated from without. *Oo* is of dream. When you dream, you are surprised by your dream, and yet the dream is you. You as subject are surprised by yourself as object. You seem to be two, you and your dream, but you are one. So subject and object, though they seem to be two, are the same. I and you are the same. This is the breakthrough of the metaphysical realization that the two that seem to be separate are really one. This is the midway point to transcendence, realizing the relationship as identity. The objects of dream are subtle objects,

self-radiant, changing form rapidly—dream, vision, god. The gods and heavens and hells are what might be called the cosmic aspect of dream. The dream is the personal aspect of myth. Dream and myth are of the same order. They are of the order of *oo*, dream consciousness. You and your god are one, just as you and your dream are. But your god isn't my god, so don't try to push it on me. Every one has his own being and consciousness.

The third order then is *mmm*, which is deep, dreamless sleep. Consciousness is there. The heart is ticking. The body will respond to heat and cold.

But waking consciousness, the *aham* consciousness, the ego-consciousness, is not in touch with pure consciousness. It is wiped out by darkness. The goal of yoga is to bring your waking consciousness into that field of *mmm*, awake. Then what it will experience is undifferentiated consciousness, not the consciousness of any thing, but that primary consciousness to which we are trying to "yoga," to link, our waking consciousness. That's what we're talking about.

The deity in the Sanskrit system representative of this is Shiva as the dancer. Look at the shape here, the arms and the head. And then look at

om. In other words, while looking at the image of Shiva, you are hearing the syllable *om,* the sound of the radiance. Now, when lecturing to Methodists about graven images, I tell them this is a permanent meditation. It's not idolatry. You're not idolizing this image; it's the opening to the radiance. Shiva helps you go through Shiva, you don't stop with him. He dances on the little dwarf Forgetfulness, is fascinated by the serpent of the world and ignorant of the fact of this weight on his back, just as we all are. But Shiva is right there, waiting for us to recognize him.

Cakra 4 is the heart cakra. This is the cakra of this transformation. The little foyer is the foyer of the wish-fulfilling tree. As the energies and as the illumination begin to approach this breakthrough, one has the feeling, "All my wishes are about to be realized." And they are. The crucial thing here is the center, where again we have the *yoni.* The last time we saw it with the *lingam* within it was at Cakra 1. But this is the golden *lingam-yoni* of the virgin birth. This is the yoni of the birth of the spiritual as opposed to the merely physical life, a new trajectory of ideas that no animal can have. With the notion of a spiritual life, the first three cakras fall into a secondary position. People can go so far, as I said, going up that *pingalā,* line, as to reject altogether their bodies which have fallen into a secondary place. The problem is to come

to this realization through the body, so that it's *in* the body that the spiritual life is realized. The animal here is an antelope, or a gazelle, which is the vehicle of Prana, the Lord of the Wind, the breath. This is the place where breath takes over and is in charge.

Two triangles form the six-pointed star. The first represents aspiration. You have heard the syllable *om* resounding through all things. You don't have to go anywhere, it's here, it's here. *Om.* That's the sense of the inward-turned meditation. "I've got it within me. The fire is here, it's there, but I don't have to go there to capture it. I am there in this." The experience of the sound of *om* is ubiquitous. And now you want to hear the sound di-

rectly, not simply through things, but directly. That is the aspiration, then, of spiritual striving. The lower triangle pointing down is inertia, physical inertia.

So now we are going to have a system of symbols of trying to put down the inertia system, the cravings of the mere physical body, so that a spiritual realization and amplification can be realized, and the energy can be carried on up. That's the center of transformation.

The next, Cakra 5, is *visuddha.* The word means "purgation," the purging of the merely animal, physical system. Or rather, not purging it so much as sublimating it, making it open up, so that through its experiences the transcendent can be experienced. Cakra 5 is at the throat. The petals are of the same dark, threatening color as those of Cakra 3. In other words, and here's the whole secret, the energy that was formerly projected out to conquering others is now turned back against yourself. This is called the turning about of the *shakti*. The *shakti*, your energy, is not facing outward anymore, but facing inward. These representations of the Yab-Yum, the male deity in embrace with the female, are the turning about of the *shakti*. It's all right here. They say that God created the world in order to enjoy himself, and the world must turn toward him. So there we are.

We had the red fiery *yoni* in Cakra 3. Here it is of ether, and our elephant has come on up. The syllable is *ham*. Having come to Cakra 4, we've taken the energy of Cakra 3 and pulled it up to Cakra 5, against ourselves.

We have the deity putting down the physical man. That's the sense of these things in Tibet and China and Japan, wherever we have Mahāyāna. The necklace of severed heads means "We're cutting off the body." We have weapons and the flower of the new life that comes from having killed the old.

Our highest god is our highest obstruction. It represents the consummation of the highest thoughts and feelings you can have. Go past that.

Meister Eckhart says, "The ultimate leave-taking is the leaving of god [that is to say, the folk god] for god [that is to say, the elementary idea]." This breakthrough is very difficult. In her hand is the head of Brahma, the creator of the world. We're going past that, and all its values.

Kali also appears with nine elephants on her shashlick, impaled human beings on her tusks, and her hand raised in the *abhaya mudrā*, meaning "Do not be afraid." We address her thus as "Our dear Mother." Shiva is sometimes represented with five heads, the five senses brought to a point.

And so through our effort, we have come to the vision of God, Cakra 6, *ājñā*, "authority or power." The soul beholds its object. What has happened? We have a two-petaled lotus, the soul and its god, Jiva and Ishvara. The goddess Hakini, on the soul of her own love, is the dominant figure here. This is Māyā with six heads. The sixth head is mind. In her six hands are the tick of time, "do not be afraid," meditation, the scriptures, "boon-bestowing," and the severed head of the creator of the world. The energy of Cakra 3 was brought to Cakra 5. Through its exercise we've broken through, and the energy of love, of Cakra 2, is now experienced in its sublime form of love for God.

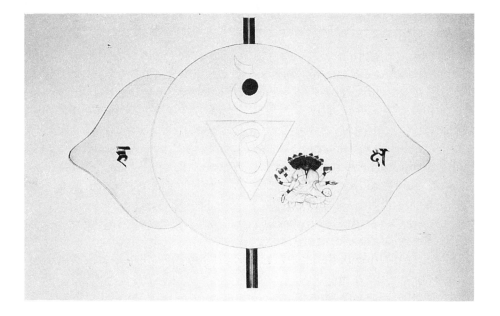

When Dante beheld Beatrice, it was in the way not of Cakra 2 but of Cakra 6. He saw her not as an object of lust but as a manifestation of the beauty of God's grace and love for the world. Through contemplating her in that way he was brought to the throne of final realization. That's what we have taking place here.

High on a wall at Elephanta Cave is a representation of Shiva as the *bindu*, as the drop striking the field of time, breaking into the pairs of opposites: Cakra 3, aggression, Cakra 2, erotics, male and female, pairs of opposites in all the aspects.

Now comes the final event, Cakra 7, *sahasrāra*. The soul beholds God, but the aim of the mystic is to be one with its beloved. "I and the father are one" (John 10:30). Halaj, the great Sufi mys-

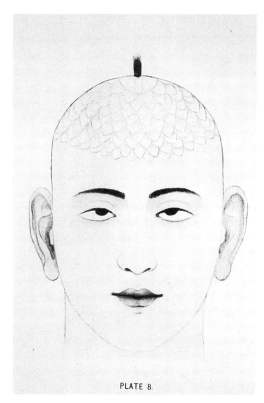

PLATE 8.

167

tic, describes the situation this same way. Ramakrishna says, "When you behold god you are not god." There is a pane of glass between. The soul beholds its object, but the goal is to be one with that. How can we break through? How can we remove that barrier and join soul and God? We're beyond pairs of opposites.

Halaj says the situation is like that of a moth seeing at night a lantern, and it wants to get to the flame. But the glass keeps it out. It batters itself all night long, and then goes to its friends in the morning and tells them what a wonderful thing it has just seen. They say, "You don't look the better for it." This is the condition of the yogi, the ascetic knocking himself to pieces to get through. The moth goes back the next night and, by luck or device, does break through. For an instant he has achieved his goal and is the flame. That instant is an eternal instant beyond time and space. That is the goal here, to remove the barrier. Bang!

In Cakra 7, *sahasrāra*, the serpent becomes one with the thousand-petaled lotus at the crown of the head. *Sahasrāra* means "thousand petaled." In the center all we see are two footprints. These are the footprints of Vishnu, which are to be worshiped. Why do we have footprints here? We thought we had broken through. They are symbols, and words can act as bar-

riers. We can get stuck with the footprints, or we can pass through. There's a saying that appears both in Lao-tzu's work and in the Upanishads. "Those who know do not speak. And those who speak do not know." That's hard for one giving a lecture, but it's a warning that we've got to go past the footprints.

Cakras 4, 5, 6, and 7 appear on a ninth-century stone cross in Northern Ireland. As early as the fourteenth century B.C. in Egypt, 1, 2, and 3 are depicted at the weighing of the heart against a feather. The monster has his nose right between Cakras 3 and 4. If the spiritual wins, then Thot is the victor, and he is in charge of Cakras 4, 5, 6, and 7.

So we come to the final problem. What is this thing between Cakra 6 and Cakra 7? At 6, from Brahma down to the blade of grass, all is pairs of opposites. This is called *māyā*, which is, as it were, the womb. It's from a root, *mā*, which means "to measure forth." So she is the one that creates all pairs of opposites, creates both the *lingam* and the *yoni*. Above that, there is neither you nor God. There is nothing of the kind. The whole universe is the goddess. We are here, hell is down there, heaven is up there. How do you go to hell? You make your ego system harder and harder and harder and are stuck with it. Hell is the place of people stuck on themselves. How do you get to heaven? Open and open and open until finally all is transpersonal.

Shiva is the god, creating the world. *Shave* means "corpse." The corpses in India, when they are about to be burned, are clothed in a yellow garment. Monks wear the yellow garment, meaning "I am a corpse. I have cut myself off from the world."

One, Two, Three, Four, Five, Six, Seven. If we stay up there the body drops off, and we are released from life. The ideal, from the point of view of someone interested in life, is to come back to the heart where the two are together, to Cakra 4, where we realize that the energy of Cakra 3 has functioned at 5, the energy of 2 at 6, and the energy of 1 at 7. Thus we know how to translate our earthly ex-perience into the spiritual exercise. Cakra 3—what we are to conquer is ourselves and our attachment and go off to the war. Cakra 2—through our human love we are to experience the radiance of eternity.

The Buddha functions from the heart center. The energy comes right from the heart center. When the Buddha says "No" to the tempter, his hand is in the earth-touching posture. But when he has experienced what is to be experienced, his hand turns around and bestows boons. And so the Buddha returns to bestow boons, returns from his austerities to teach. The lord of the universe himself bows to and embraces himself as the universe, the goddess. So that's the lesson of the Kundalini.

Then, in 1959, Buddhism in Tibet was extinguished by the Chinese invasion. But in the interval, there was preserved in Tibet, as though in a pickling jar, the Buddhist forms of the highest, most sophisticated Tantric developments.

Now the mythology of death and birth is of reincarnation. Reincarnation is the counterpart in the Orient of purgatory in the West. That is to say, it is a chance to live again, to live out the experiences that should have illuminated you. Purgatory, as I like to say, is a postgraduate course; if you die unilluminated, unready to behold the beatific vision which would smash everything that you are if you haven't opened, it's there to purge you. And so, in the Orient, you come back for another lifetime.

Between the moment of death and the moment of reconception, forty-nine days pass—seven times seven days. During the course of this, you go through all the worlds of the cakras, the cakra system that was introduced in the previous chapters, except you go in the opposite direction—from top to bottom. At the moment of death, you experience the great light. Can you stand it? Have you prepared yourself to dissolve? If you haven't, there's immediate pullback, protection. That starts you down.

The family of the moribund will have sent for a lama, a priest, probably their family chaplain and teacher, to be present. He will see to it that the person about to die takes the posture of the Buddha for the *parinirvāna*, the lion posture. He will have his hand on the jugular vein, or the pulse, so that he will know the precise moment of death. He will then begin to instruct.

You may ask, "What's the point of instructing somebody who's dead about the journey that the soul is about to take?" There are two aspects to this. One aspect is: Does a person die completely, all at once? Is there not a jangling, dying of the nerves? Apparently the body does not die all at once. So the idea that the steadying voice of one who has been your teacher will help you to survive that jangling moment of disintegration of the spirit, so that you will hold to the spirit and know where you are on the way.

The other aspect, since the family is present, is that this is a meditation on death. This is a good thing to have happen. You have come in your family life to an immediate and intense experience of one of the great experiences, the experience of death and its meaning, or its sense, for your life. The lama will consequently be using this as a meditation moment for the family, instead of just sitting around talking about "how he was in the old days."

At the moment of death the lama will say, "You are now experiencing the mother light; between your consciousness and universal consciousness, no obstruction. Try to hold that. . . ." But you've missed it.

So you have started at the top and, being unable to hold, you've come down, now to *ājñā*, Cakra 6. The lama will now say, "Try to bring into your consciousness the image of the lord that has been of your worship throughout your lifetime." This may be any god, so long as that god has been understood to be the supreme image of the powers of the energizing energies of the universe as they have operated in your lifetime. It may be a Buddha image of one or another, as we'll see, or it may be one of the Hindu gods. It may be some notion of Allah. It may be Yahweh. Any deity that's been your top deity, this is the place to contemplate it. He's second. He's not top, he's second. If you can't hold to that, there comes a very interesting series of experiences at Cakra 5, the next cakra.

There are two stages here. Before your ego has solidified, you are open to the radiance, in descending series, of those five Buddhas that represent the center and the four directions. They will be experienced in sequence: first, the Buddha of the center, and then the Buddhas of the east, south,

west, and north. If none of these radiances has been able to hold you, but you have been frightened of all, it's because you are still holding much too tightly to your ego. These same five Buddhas will then turn into their wrathful aspect. They will seem horrific. They will seem terrifying. They will be there to smash your ego with terror. If this doesn't work, we come down still another stage—we're still at Cakra 5—and there comes what is called the knowledge-holding aspect of these deities.

Some people are unable to experience radiance, but they can listen to a lecture. I think it was Oscar Wilde who said, "An American, if he was given a chance to choose between going to heaven and hearing a lecture about heaven, he'd go to the lecture." So you're unable to experience heaven, but perhaps you'll take a lecture about it. Maybe that'll save you.

Down to this point you have been beyond the level of fear of death. That comes at the heart cakra, Cakra 4. And now you come into that place of the upward and downward pointed triangles—the place of decision and choice. This is a critical one. The lama will be telling you where you are on the way down and what to hold to and to try to do it; and here you are disintegrating, trying to have this realization that will release you from another birth.

Finally we get down to Cakra 3. Now come the terrors of death. Before this, death has been the ornament of life, which it is. Life without death in it is no life at all. It's just a fixture. But it's the process of death in you that is life, the burning. Down to here death has been celebrated; everyone is saying, "Kill, kill, kill! Oh wow, isn't this wonderful!" And then down here it all changes. This is the moment of decision, a moment of great terror. And the lama will say, "Do not be afraid. These powers that are tearing you apart are just figments of your own imagination. They are in the field of time, figments. Hold. There's nothing to lose. There's nothing to do. Hold the stillpoint without moving." But you've lost it. Great cliffs close behind you, and the upper regions are lost to you. You are now caught in the descent through the last three cakras. But I don't want to give away the whole story, so let's start our passage.

We begin with the Bodhisattva Avalokiteshvara, the Bodhisattva of Infinite Compassion. His compassion reaches to the abyss of hell. There is no being and there is no deed that is beyond the reach of his compassion. This is the Bodhisattva who is living among us incarnate in the Dalai Lama, who is regarded as an incarnation of the Bodhisattva Avalokiteshvara of Infinite Compassion. Now I've heard the

Dalai Lama lecture, and his accent always, in his talks about Buddhism, is on the force of compassion and mercy and love. There are many ways, but this is the way of the Bodhisattva and the way of the tradition that we're now talking about. This is an eighteenth-century Dalai Lama, the Bodhisattva Avalokiteshvara looking down in mercy at the lotus of the world. The Dalai Lamas lived in the Potala, the gigantic palace complex on a hill overlooking Lhasa. This is the counterpart of Olympus with the palace of the gods on the top, that mythic image of the world axis where heaven and earth come together. The Bodhisattva represents the incarnation on earth of the quality of divine mercy from heaven. People in the old days used to take their daily walks around the palace in the clockwise direction, circumambulation. They'd take with them their pet lambs and dogs. It's the one life that inhabits the whole world, so they, too, could build up merit by circumambulating. What a lovely thing. The animals are little fellows coming along, and they'll be up there later. This is true also of the trees and the grass and even the rocks. Well, that's now finished. The Potala is now a museum.

So, to begin again, a person is about to die. The local lama has his hand on the pulse. At the moment of death he says, "You are now beholding the

mother light." That is absolute Brahma, undifferentiated consciousness; that's what we're intending all the way here. You may speak of it as the void, you may speak of it as the abyss, you may speak of it as mother light. It is that which transcends all cogitations. There are no words for it. So he will say, "Hold." If you can't, you slip down now from Cakra 7 to 6 and he asks you to bring to consciousness the image of the lord that you have chosen for your life contemplation.

This beautiful figure is Mahāvairochana, the Great Sun Buddha; in Japanese, Dainichi-nyorai, Great-Day-Just-Come. The five meditation Buddhas are in his tiara. In my book *The Mythic Image* I have a picture of this Buddha. When starting to write about it, I thought, Who am I to write about Dainichi-nyorai? Dante has already done it, in the last canto of *The Divine Comedy*. Mahāvairochana is like the Trinity: one divine substance, but in five aspects instead of three divine personalities—representing the power, the consciousness, and the rapture of the divine—seated or appearing in the heavenly rose, or on the lotus. Dante, beholding the Trinity, the personification of the mystery, saw three rings of light.

Finnegans Wake begins with the second half of the sentence with which the book ends: "A way a lone a last a loved a long the . . ." ". . . riverrun, past Eve and Adam's, from swerve of shore to bend of bay, brings us by a commodius vicus of recirvulation back to Howth Castle and Environs." Well, you can quit here—"A way a lone a last a loved a long the . . ." I'm finished with the book, I'm out. Or, gee, I enjoyed that book, I'd like to do it again. You see, you're back. That's reincarnation.

We're now going to descend to Cakra 5, the throat cakra, where you encounter the benevolent manifestations of the five meditation Buddhas. First, at the center, there appears the bliss-bestowing Buddha, Vairochana, the "Sun Buddha," seated in meditation at the immovable spot of illumination, doing nothing. There is such bliss as you are afraid to accept. The pig of ignorance has been slain; the teaching has been communicated to the disciples. The Buddha in teaching posture represents doing something to help you. You haven't got there, you haven't reached the top, but you are pretty close. A word of instruction may suddenly do it for you.

If you allow the vision of Vairochana to fade, then from the east appears Akshobhya, meaning "can't be moved." He's at the immovable spot. He has illumination, so the tempter cannot move him. In his hand he will have the

thunderbolt, the *vajra*, and he will be embracing his *shakti* Mamaki—that is, "turning about" his energy, his *shakti*, to the aim of illumination. Your vice is your virtue. The quality here is tenacity, and the negative aspect of tenacity is stubbornness. If your virtue is stubbornness, hold it, don't lose it. This is one of the problems of renovating one's character.

The psychological problem in the play *Equus*, which the pychiatrist realized, was that in "healing" his patient, he had deprived him of his God. I think it's Nietzsche who said, "Be careful, lest in casting out your devil, you cast out the best thing that's in you." Many people who have been psychoanalyzed are like filleted fish. Their character is gone.

If you are nasty, be nasty, but turn around the energy, the *shakti*. If stubbornness is all you've got and you haven't turned it around, you will be reborn in the realm of the stubborn. That's hell. Hell is the place of people who are stubborn about their individuations and about what those individuations mean to them, their personalities, their wishes, their notions of good and evil, and so forth. So this is your virtue and your vice.

Fudo, the Japanese God of Wisdom, is Akshobhya in the aspect of "immovable in fire." The picture in the *New York Times* of the Vietnamese monk

who set himself on fire was a picture of Fudo. There he was seated, immovable in fire. If he had moved, he would have lost merit. The point is, he transcended his body so he could do a thing like that. It's impudence to do that when you can't do that.

If you are holding onto the thunderbolt of illumination, responding to Vairochana's teaching, and you are still to be reborn, you will be reborn in heaven. If you are stuck with your stubbornness, you will be reborn in hell. The Buddha sits immovable, in the earth-touching posture, at that moment when life is speaking to him in its loudest voice, and he is deaf to it. He is going to the father—to the crucifixion.

If this opportunity fades, there arises from the south the most charming of these Buddhas, Ratnasambhava, "born of a jewel." Embraced by his *shakti* "Buddha-Eyes," his quality is beauty. And what's the vice? Pride. If your pride is in your beauty, hold to it, but turn it about, so that the beauty that you are proud of is your spiritual beauty. Then you will cultivate that. Do not get rid of your vice. If it's pride, make the pride work to your illumination, not to your degradation. That's all there is to this. If you are reborn under the sign of this deity, you will have a human rebirth. So now we have had three of the realms of rebirth

—heaven, hell, and human. The Lord of the South is boon-bestowing, generous. The proud and the beautiful are generous.

If the vision of this saving Buddha pair fades, from the west arises the favorite Buddha of the Far East, Amida. In Sanskrit, he's Amitabha—*a-mita* means "immeasurable"; *ābha* is "radiance"—the Buddha of Immeasurable Radiance. There's a legend associated with his name. When he was on the very threshold of illumination he made a vow. "I will not accept illumination for myself unless, through my illumination, I can bring to illumination and release all beings who pay me worship, who honor my name."

So when he achieved illumination, there appeared before him a great lake, a lake of bliss, and on the lake were lotuses. Anyone who has during his lifetime paid devotion to Amida will not be committed to another lifetime but will be reborn on a lotus in Amida's lake in *sukhāvatī,* the "Land of Bliss." If the person was not even close to illumination at the point of death, he'll be reborn in a closed lotus floating on waters of five colors, the colors of the five elements. And as the waters ripple, he'll hear, "All is impermanent; all is without self." And around the lake will be jeweled trees, with jeweled birds singing, "All is impermanent; all is without a self." And musical instruments in the air will be playing, "All is impermanent; all is without a self." Meanwhile the radiance of the Buddha himself, like the setting sun on the western horizon, will be penetrating the petals. Finally, the person will get the message, the petals will open, and there he will be, sitting as a Buddha in meditation, floating on the lotus pond. And presently in his meditation he will dissolve into a rapture and transcendence.

Amitabha is the Buddha whose lieutenant is Avalokiteshvara and whose incarnation on earth, then, is in the Dalai Lama. Embraced by his *shakti,* known as the "Woman in White," his quality is mercy, compassion. And what do you suppose the vice would be? Attachment—attachment to that being for whom you feel love. If you die with that attachment you will be reborn in the world of the hungry ghosts. They have ravenous bellies and pinpoint mouths, so they can never eat what they desire.

If Amitabha and his *shakti* fade, the fourth of the surrounding Buddhas appears from the north, the ominous direction. His name is Amoghasiddhi, "He who will not be turned from the achievement of his aim." *Siddhi* is "aim," or "achievement." *Amogha* is "not to be distracted from it."

The virtue here is tenacity of purpose, not simply holding to where you

are but holding with conscious intention. The negative aspect is belligerence, and if you die in this context, you will be reborn in the realm of the antigods, the demons, the fighting gods.

What has happened is, as we've come down we've lost, as it were, the *vajra* that Akshobhya had in his hand, and now we're in quest of it. So there's a descending series here. This is the great Tibetan representation of the *vajra* with the yin-yang in the center. There is a Chinese and Hindu combination here.

Still at cakra 5, we descend another

step to encounter a great mandala of dancers, the Knowledge-Holding Deities. They are having a ball. I think of it as a kind of college prom. They are shouting, "Death! Death! Death!"; waving banners made of flayed human skins; and blowing trumpets made of human thigh bones. Death is the ornament of life. They are not afraid of death. They are right on the edge, still experiencing the excitement of dying.

The mandala is a terrific affair. The gods that were formerly benevolent—Vairochana, Akshobhya, and so forth—are dancing with female figures known as Dakinis, sort of space fairies. I once saw on Forty-second Street an advertisement for the movie *Firewomen of Outer Space*. That's what we've got here. In one hand is a flaying knife with a thunderbolt handle. There is a staff with heads on it and a thunderbolt, and necklace of skulls. Such is the kind that you meet at these parties. The lion-headed Dakini, Sima-dakini, tramples the mere animal nature. In fact, every time one accepts a partner like that, one has trampled on one's own animal nature. Compassion has taken over. The great one is Sarva-Buddha Dakini, a kind of fairy goddess, of all the Buddhas. And what does she drink from? The top of a skull. And what does she drink? Blood. She wears a kilt made of carved

human bones and carries a thunderbolt flaying knife.

The inspiration for many of these images is Kali, the Hindu goddess of the same power. She has been taken over in the Buddha system by these Dakinis, the partners in this dance. Death is being celebrated at this stage. You are dancing in partnership with Lady Death, and you don't mind. But if you die caught up in the dance, instead of in its significance, you will be reborn as an animal.

Then come the deities in their ferocious aspects, their wrathful aspects. The lama at the bedside will say, "The deities will be coming to you, every hair on their heads radiant with fire, and they will be making strange sounds: '*kla, kla, kla.*' Do not be terrified. These are but the violent aspect of your own consciousness." Your whole being is terror and fright, but the lama will be saying, "Do not be terrified, do not move." This is the second temptation of the Buddha, the temptation of fear and terror. "Be calm."

One remains calm by holding to Yama-Antaka, that aspect of the powers that kills in you the fear of death. Yama is the Lord Death, the first man who died. *Antaka* means "end"—the ender of the fear of death, the ender of the Lord Death. He is surrounded by various powers. There is a female who is a convert to Buddhism, and she goes out to convert everybody else. Like all converts she is a little bit insecure and wants to reassure herself by converting everybody else. People who would not submit, she flayed. Her name is Lhamo. The first person she could not convert, and so flayed, was her own son. In one representation she is in such a fury that you can't even see her. The peacock-feathered parasol is her sign. There is a violent aspect—of the power to break the ego.

So we've come down now, from the top through Cakra 6 to Cakra 5, where the syllable is *ham*, and now we're coming down to Cakra 4, at the level of the heart, where the syllable is *yam*, and you see the two triangles. This is the place of decision. If you don't sign out here, you're going to come down the rest of the way. This is the place of the moon. The moon is both body and light, and so are you below this level. Now are you going to identify with the body, the vehicle, or are you going to identify with the light?

You'll see the lunar horns and monster buffalo face of Yama. The lama will be saying, "You have come to the realm of the Lord Death, the judge of the dead. His minions will come at you, and they will tear you apart."

Here is a tanka representing this realm where the Lord Death presides over people being judged. All of this now, is what has come upon you. At the weighing scales, good deeds are weighed against bad deeds, and then people are assigned to the different worlds. You can see the hell-tortures: people being chopped to pieces, others being dragged to a freezing hell, some who are boiling. Notice the book, and what happens to monks who skip passages in their prayers. The fellow with the heavy rock on his back is a person who likes to kill insects. There are more horrific scenes of subtle terrors, but the lama will be saying, "Do not be afraid."

I thought about this when I read of the gross terrors—the actual torture scenes—that had occurred in Tibet in 1959. Monks were being torn apart, sometimes for as long as seven days, without being killed. Thousands of other monks were killed, just as when the Muslims came into north India. Monasteries around Lhasa that had six or eight thousand monks were wiped out. And I thought, if a monk there, having all this happen, could think, "Nothing is happening, it's merely the field of time, the stillpoint is here," then he would achieve illumination.

When Mansur al-Hallaj, the great Sufi mystic, was about to be tortured and crucified as Jesus was, he is said to have uttered this prayer, "O Lord, if you had revealed to them what you have revealed to me, they would not

184

be doing this to me. If you had not revealed to me what you have, this would not be happening to me. O Lord, praise to thee and thy works.'' That's big stuff. Hallaj is also reported to have said, ''The function of the orthodox community is to give the mystic his desire.'' That's a good way—a heroic way—to think about it.

So we're in the realm of the Lord Judge of the Dead, the bull with the moon horns, and the terrors. If we can get past this, we are released. If we can't, there closes behind us a great cliff, and the sublime is no longer ours. And we hear noises, the noises of the world. Sometimes when you hear these noises, try not to think of what is being said, but of what is talking. What is talking is ignorance, lust, and malice. The world as it's experienced by people who are still in fear of the Lord Death is a world of the first three cakras: ignorance, lust, and malice. The great cliff is the boundary beyond which we do not see because we are in fear of the Lord Death.

So, we've slipped. We're on the last three cakras now. At Cakra 3, you begin to see couples embracing. And the lama at your side will be saying, ''Try not to get between them.'' So we've come to the level of Dr. Freud. Below here, we've already gotten between them and we're going to be born, either as male or as female. If we

are born male, we will find ourselves hating our father and loving our mother. If we are born female, it will be the other way around. The Oedipus and the Electra complexes.

And so, the final job of the lama is to get you born into a decent environment, where you have a chance to receive Buddhist instructions for another lifetime, and to save you from birth, let's say, in the egg of a flea, the womb of a mouse, or something like that. All of these are possibilities.

Then you are born, a frightened, terrified little thing, who's just had a great fight through the birth canal. And your eyes open to the surfaces of things, for you have been through the whole inward mystery and have forgotten it.

Plato, in the *Timaeus*, says, ''The only thing one can do for another is reintroduce him to those forms of the spirit, the memory of which was lost at birth.'' But how we do this is the problem.

In a mandala made by one of Jung's patients, you have the six worlds, and in the middle she is shown reading—undoubtedly reading Jung. I thought this was a very interesting mandala, particularly because of the reading aspect.

This is Pancaksara, the patroness of books, coming to illumination through reading scriptures. When you have

been led by scripture not to fear death anymore, that world which seemed such a horror is transformed into a world of Buddha consciousness —Buddha everywhere. It's through scripture that one has been led to this. Now this figure, Pancaksara, is an *Idam*, which means "chosen deity" —the deity that you yourself have chosen—*istadevata*, the "wished-for deity."

This is a very sophisticated idea. Such a deity has no existence. It's a picture. It's to put in your mind the idea of a deity, and it will achieve life insofar as you make this your deity. This deity then becomes the guide of your life.

I speak first of Pancaksara, the deity of reading and scripture, because it happens to be my *idam*. Everything I know I have gotten from reading. When I meet Buddhas and yogis and whatnot I interpret them in terms of my reading. I put this *idam* right on the face of the Buddha himself. This is what holds me.

Other people will have other *istadevatas*, other chosen deities, but stick to your chosen deity. It's your way, and the whole Buddha world will come to your knowledge through whatever your deity is.

Kalacakra is another *istadevata* or *idam*. *Kalacakra* means "the wheel of time." Everything is Buddha. This is the world which, when you are in fear of death, is such a horrible place. But no horror can survive the radiance of these knowledges that come.

I once had a *tanka* of Sakra Samvararaja, the All-Embracing Lord, hanging in the foyer in my apartment. I was helping a Tibetan monk write his autobiography, and as he walked out of the apartment he saw the *tanka* and said, "Why that's the *istadevata* of my monastery." So an *idam* can be not simply a personal choice, but the power informing the exercises of an entire monastery. This is the most sophisticated notion of deity anywhere that I know of, this notion of a chosen deity that is going to be your guide.

And so with this idea, we come to the conclusion of this story of how the Lord, with his *shakti* turned about, comes to transcendence—becomes the Buddha, immovable, teaching the world.

10

From Darkness to Light: The Mystery Religions of Ancient Greece

The essence of the spiritual experience intended by the mystery religions of Classical Greece was the shifting of consciousness from the purely phenomenal aspect of one's life to the spiritual, the deep, the energetic, eternal aspect. Some of the many, many associated rituals began back in the Bronze Age. With the coming of the Homeric patriarchal warrior people, they moved into the background for a while, but later they came forward again.

The mysteries of Eleusis—a wonderful shrine just west of Athens that was a sacred spot for the Athenians—date from the Bronze Age. Eleusis flourished in the Classical world and survived in Roman times until the conversion of the Roman Empire into a Christian empire. Under Constantine, around A.D. 327 or so, Christianity was recognized as one of the permitted religions in the Roman Empire. Very shortly thereafter, with Theodosius, Christianity—but only the specific form of Christianity practiced by the Byzantine throne—was declared to be the only permitted religion in the Roman Empire. And so began a system of violent persecution and vandalism of shrines, and the more sacred the shrine, the more violent the damage. The destruction of Eleusis in A.D. 395 is a good example of what happened.

Prior to that spiritual crisis in Western civilization, however, during the Hellenistic period, many of the earlier mystery cults had come back into manifestation.

It's my belief that St. Paul's great insight on the road to Damascus was that the death of Jesus Christ on the cross could be interpreted in terms of the mystery religions' understanding of the death and the resurrection of the savior—that is, as the death of one's purely material, animal existence and the birth, then, of the spiritual life. This is symbolized in Christian terminology by the transformation of the old Adam into the new Adam. Then we have the refrain of *O felix culpa*, "O happy fault"—original sin—and the notion that the fall of man into the field of time out of the timeless rapture of Eden was followed by the coming of the Savior, who represented a sublimation—a higher manifestation of the consciousness of humanity than that which had been represented in the garden—and so, without the fall, there would have been no savior. Well, all of this is really mystic language from the Greek mysteries.

We actually know very little about the Greek mystery religions because they did remain mysteries. No one was allowed to betray or talk about what went on in the inner sanctuaries. We have to depend on outside observations, some by people like Clement of Alexandria who were attacking the classical mysteries. From them we can glean something of what the rituals were like, but I think the best evidence is in the art—the ceramics, sculpture, and so forth—which provides small clues that convey some sense of what the rituals intended and what their forms might have been.

In the classical world, the planting time was in the fall, the harvest was in the spring, and the fruits of the harvest, the grains, were stored in silos in the ground during the fierce heat of the summer for planting again the following fall. Consequently, the richness, the wealth of the community, was in the keep of the underworld, in the keep of the chthonic underworld divinity, Pluto. This votive tablet from

fifth-century Athens shows Athena giving the grain to Pluto in his aspect as *puer eternis*, the eternal boy.

A deity like Pluto—Merlin in the Celtic stories—can be represented either as a youth or as an old man, the aged one. He is frequently pictured with a cornucopia, the bounty of our life in his keep. Athena sits near a serpent like the one in the Indian seal from 3000 B.C. The mythological notion of the cult was that Eleusis was the place where grain agriculture was first invented by Demeter, the goddess of the telluric earth. That's just a mythological idea. We all know that Eleusis was not the place where grain agriculture originated, but for the cult, it was.

The notion that it's out of the darkness of the abyss, the chthonic realm, that life comes is an important mythological motif. And so these cults were very much associated with a cycle of death, descent into the underworld, and then life reborn again. By analogy, this was symbolized in the agricultural cycle of the harvest death, the planting of seed, and the plants coming to life again. In other words, agricultural imagery was used to render a spiritual message.

This is from a vase in a museum in Brussels. The candidate for illumination is being received by the *psycho-*

pompos, the guide of the sanctuary. On the right stands a figure, and the club beside him tells us who it is: Herakles, or Hercules, and we're going to see him in an interesting situation a little later in the ceremonial adventure. And so, carrying a torch—which means we're going into the dark realm—the candidate is conducted into the shrine.

This sarcophagus, from a palace in Rome, shows step by step something of what went on in these ceremonies. On the left is a laurel tree, which is *apotropaic;* that is to say, it defends the threshold against evil presences. It has a sanctifying power as a threshold tree. Beside it is an aspect of Bacchus —or Dionysos, it's the same deity— known as Iacchus, which is the cry of greeting that was uttered at a certain moment in the ceremony when the revelation of the new birth was rendered. Iacchus stands by an altar bearing the fruits of offering, and he holds a torch, which—again—always indicates the underworld, or chthonic, adventure.

In the center are the two great goddesses—Demeter, seated on the sacred basket with the serpent, and her daughter, Persephone, the one who dies and is resurrected, who is abducted and then returns—the *Anodos* and *Kathodos* of the maiden. The torch of Demeter is held upward, purifying the upper regions. That of Persephone is downward, purifying the lower. So this is a purification passage, and in this cult these two are going to be the dominant figures—the dual goddess —the goddess of life and the goddess of the underworld, out of which new life comes.

In the tableau on the right we see the candidate with his head covered, for he is going to experience a revelation, an epiphany—the showing forth of the mystery to a person who experiences it for the first time. The guide is pouring offerings, and facing him is Bacchus-Dionysos. The figure behind him is Hecate, the dark, negative aspect of the goddess, often associated with witchcraft.

Some very interesting research concerning the plants associated with these cults has shown that the people who were going to go through the great ceremony consumed a barley drink before attending the rites. One of the historically important hallucinogens is ergot, which is produced by a fungus that grows parasitically on barley. Since one family was for centuries in charge of the rites, many now believe that this barley broth contained a bit of ergot. There is a very fine study called *The Road to Eleusis,* written by Albert Hofmann, who discovered LSD; R. Gordon Wasson; and classical scholar Carl A. P. Ruck. This book deals with the entire ritual of Eleusis in detail as a ceremonial matching of the rapturous state of the people who have taken the drink with a theatrical performance that is rendered as an epiphany. So there's an inward readiness and an outer fulfillment. Socrates himself is reported to have spoken about the importance to him of the experience at Eleusis. Something in the way of a revelation was actually experienced there.

Now the story of Persephone, the daughter of Demeter, is that she's out picking flowers in the spring, and suddenly Hades appears in his chariot and carries her off to the underworld. Just as Isis was bereaved of Osiris, so Demeter is of Persephone. She goes to find her lost daughter. When Demeter comes to Eleusis, she sits down by a well, just as Isis sat down by the well outside the palace where her husband's body and sarcophagus were enclosed in the pillar. That well at Eleusis is still there, at least a reconstruction of it.

The people come out to the well and try to comfort Demeter, but she is disconsolate until a little creature named Baubo does an obscene dance, and then Demeter has to laugh, that's all she can do. This is a wonderful motif —the obscenity provides another perspective. You move out of the sphere of the developed person, back into the sphere of the nature dynamics of generation and regeneration, and are released from the bondage of your grief.

An equivalence to Persephone is the golden stalk of wheat. Clement of Alexandria mocks the Eleusinian mysteries and says what a silly thing to have the culminating moment be that of the elevation of a grain of wheat. Yet the culmination of the Roman Catholic mass is the elevation of a wafer of wheat. It's not the object, it's the reference that is the sense of a ritual. Any object can become the center of the cult. At Eleusis, the central cultic object was the wonderful food plant, which nourishes our physical life and, when consumed with the understanding that it is a divine gift, our spiritual life as well.

In the earliest primitive rites associated with food plants, the typical underlying myth is of a deity of some kind who has been killed, cut up, and buried. And out of the buried parts of the deity comes the grain or whatever the food plant. Longfellow's Hiawatha speaks of the visionary experience of a young man on a vision quest. A young deity comes to him, wrestles with him for three nights, and then on the fourth night says, "Now you're going to kill me and bury me." Hiawatha does so, and out of his buried body comes maize.

The meditation is that we are eating divine substance and this divine substance is what is feeding us. It isn't just physical substance, and that's part of the meditation: how our whole life is supported by the giving and yielding of some transcendent power.

People sometimes ask me, "What

rituals can we have?" You've got the rituals, only you're not meditating on them. When you eat a meal, that's a ritual. Just realize what you're doing. When you consult your friends, that's a ritual. Just think what you're doing. When you beget a child or give birth to a child—what more do you want?

Here is the youth Philophates, who is going to go forth with the grain. He is being blessed by Demeter and Persephone. He is the vehicle. On one side of this vase he is pictured as an old man, on his mystic vehicle, bringing the blessing of the wheat, the grain. Hermes is leading him with the caduceus as his staff. Turning this vase around, we see Dionysos with a chal-

ice, on the same vehicle, being led by a satyr. There are the bread and the wine of the mass. The rituals of the early Christian tradition were built on rituals that were already in place. So we get a sense of how rites and myths develop organically without breaking off: new readings, new vocabularies, new sophistications are brought in. This is the chalice of the mass with the blood of Dionysos, which is the wine, the transubstantiated wine. But in this ritual it doesn't have to be transubstantiated because it is already the divine wine.

Now the story of Dionysos' birth is that he was born from the thigh of Zeus. Zeus had a way of giving birth to children. He swallowed Athena's mother when he knew that she was pregnant. Then, of course, one day he has a fine headache. She has given birth, and he's got to be the medium, and he's screaming with a headache when Hephaistos, the mechanic of the gods, comes in with an axe, splits Zeus' head open, and out jumps Athena, fully born. Voilà!

We have a similar thing now with Dionysos. Semele, Dionysos' mother, had slept with Zeus, and she had the indiscretion to boast of this to Hera, Zeus' wife. Hera said, "Yes, darling, but Zeus has not revealed himself to you in the same majesty with which he has revealed himself to me." So next time Zeus comes along, Semele is sulking, and he says, "What's the matter?" She says, "Well, you haven't revealed yourself to me in the same majesty as to Hera." "Look out," he says, "you're not quite ready for this." She says, "Well, you've always told me you'd do anything I asked." So Zeus says, "All right, look out, girlie." Bang! That was the end of her.

But he was very much concerned about the fetus in her womb, and so he took it out and slit open his thigh and put Dionysos in there. So Dionysos is the "one of two wombs"—the female mother life and then the male initiation life. Then Zeus has a pain in his leg one day, and Hermes comes to receive the newly born child on a golden cloth, and he turns him over to the three nymphs. So little Dionysos is raised by the nymphs.

Here is Dionysos at the tree. Notice the serpent. Here's the whole story again. It's wonderful the way these things recur. It doesn't take too much time and study to learn this pictorial vocabulary. It's a pictorial script, and rearranging the forms rearranges the order of the experience, the depth of the experience, or the precise relevance to this or that myth.

The Apollonian religion of the Olympians—of Zeus, and so forth—was light-oriented. Dionysos represents the dynamic of the dark, and so

he's properly associated with these mystery rituals. The best discussion, in my opinion, of Dionysos and Apollo is in Nietzsche's *The Birth of Tragedy*, where they are shown in relation to the whole world of the classical arts. Nietzsche writes of Dionysos as the dynamic of time that rolls through all things, destroying old forms and bringing forth new with, what he terms is, an "indifference to the differences." In contrast to this is the light world of Apollo and its interest in the exquisite differences of forms, which Nietzsche calls the *principium individuationis.* The power of Dionysos is to ride on the full fury of the life force. That's what he represents. So, the essential message of the rites, apparently, is that of a realization in a properly prepared way of the dynamic of inexhaustible nature which pours its energy into the field of time and with which we are to be in harmony, both in its destructive and in its productive aspects. This is experience of the life power in its full career.

This picture is of Dionysos and Semele, his mother. Between them is the cup of his blood, the chalice of the mass. I am reminded of medieval pictures of the coronation of the Virgin by her son, Jesus. The two are shown at about the same age, thirty-five or so.

This golden bowl, called the Pietroasa bowl, was dug up about one hundred years ago in Rumania, with a whole hoard of gold objects. It was taken to the British Museum and reproduced. This is from the reproduction. During World War I, when the Germans were moving into Rumania, it was thought that it would be good to protect this bowl, so it was taken to Russia, where it was, of course, melted down. So we don't have it. We have to deal with the reproduction. So I've had a photograph turned into a drawing so that we can go through the story step by step. This will be our initiation.

Seated in the center of the bowl, on the basket with the vine that produces the wine that is in her chalice—

or in the Grail—is the goddess, the mother universe with the blood of her child, her son.

There are sixteen figures round-about. This is Orpheus, the fisher. The theme of the fishing of fish out of the water into the light is associated with initiation. Here we are lost in the waters of ignorance, and Orpheus the fisher will fish us out. In the Grail romances, this is a theme related to the Fisher King. In the Christian tradition, when Jesus called his apostles, who were fishermen, he said, "I will make you fishers of men." That's the same Orphic idea. The Pope's ring is known as the fisherman's ring, and on it is an engraving of the hall of fishes. So here we have Orpheus with his fishing rod and his net, and lying at his feet is a fish.

Proceeding clockwise, we see the candidate, bearing a torch. As he enters the sanctuary, he takes a pine cone from a basket on the head of a door guardian. The door guardian is represented as a small figure, simply to be able to fit the whole thing on the bowl. Part of a magnificent, full-sized statue of one of these door guardians, with the sacred basket still on her head, is in the museum at Eleusis. It's one of the pieces that was smashed by the zealots of love.

So, the candidate takes a pine cone

from the basket. Why a pine cone? It's a significant symbol. In the Vatican there is a twelve-foot-high bronze pine cone that was formerly in the Roman Field of Mars. What is it that is important in a pine cone? What is important is the seed and not the cone. And so, in each of us, what is important is the seed of consciousness which is to be released—the new Adam, the one reborn after the death of the old.

A Christian lamp of about the third century is decorated with the Jonah legend, which is symbolic of the coming of the human out of the fish condition. So you can take a legend and read into it a mystic reading which may or may not have been there in the first place. The Jonah story is that he was a missionary who was told by God to preach in Nineveh, but he fled on a ship and was a source of trouble to everyone. Evidently off center and a negative presence, he was thrown overboard and consumed by a fish, but later he came out of the fish. This motif is known as the "night sea journey." It's an old, old story. Hiawatha was consumed by a fish, the raven hero of the Northwest Coast Indians was consumed by a fish, and so forth. This is the going down into the abyss and coming out again—the same mythologies that we're dealing with here.

So our friend has taken the pine

cone and now, led by a female guide with the little pail of the elixir of immortality, he is brought to the sanctuary of the two goddesses.

Demeter, with the raven of death on her shoulder, is the one in the field of birth and death—what we call the telluric earth, the earth from which the plants grow. Beside her is Persephone, with the torch, who represents the chthonic earth, the deep caves of the abyss.

This is the first stage of his initiation. We do not know what the rites were that were associated with this pair, but we do know what the message is—to come into harmonious relationship with these two aspects of our being.

When the hero has gone through this, he is symbolically older, so he is now represented with a beard, and he's being blessed, then, by Fortuna, or Tyche. He's now completed the first grade of initiation, initiation through the goddesses.

We next see our candidate, the mystes in the aspect of youth again, about to experience the second grade of initiation, initiation into the ultimate depths. Before him is Pluto, or Hades, the god of the abyss, with a kind of alligator monster of the abyssal waters under his feet and an enormous cornucopia in his arm. In the candidate's left hand is a palm, the palm of the pilgrim, and scholars suggest that in his right hand is a poppy plant, which is associated with dream and sleep and vision. What is to be the fruit of this experience of the ultimate depth?

One of the experiences of this initiation is to be about transcendent androgyneity, the realization that we are, as beings in time, simply one fraction of what we truly are. Hence Herakles, the most macho of all the gods, is sometimes pictured in women's clothes. And so the next figure depicted is our hero as the androgyne. His hair is long, on his head are the wings of the spirit, and in his hand is an empty bowl. He is both male and female. But the sense of this final initiation is not only of the androgyneity, the transcendence of the pair of opposites of our sexual identification, but also of the recognition that our mortality and our immortality are one—the union of the lunar and the solar consciousness that I've talked about before.

Accordingly, the next two figures are the twin heroes Castor and Pollux, who are regarding each other. Castor is mortal and Pollux is immortal. And so are we, both mortal and immortal. Notice the raven of death on Castor's shoulder: we've come back, cycled around, and death is coming back to us.

Associated with each of the planets in this Ptolemaic sequence is a muse. There are nine muses, and they are clothed. Art is the clothing of a revelation. When we get up top, at the very throne of Apollo, where the revelation to which the arts are pointing is achieved, we have three graces naked. So, nine muses, and the square root of 9 is 3. When Dante beheld Beatrice, she was nine years old. At his second beholding of her, she was eighteen and so was he. And he said, "She is a nine because her root is in the Trinity." She was his muse. The muses are nine, and their root is in the Trinity, which in the Hermetic system is represented in the female form, whereas in the Christian, it is in male form—the three persons in the one substance of the divine Trinity in its mystery.

The same, unmoving substance is here personified as Apollo, male, and the moved aspects are female. The text says, "The radiance, the bliss, of the Apollonian mind moves everywhere the muses." The muses, the inspirations of poetry—which is also to say, of religion, of mythology—are moved by the radiance of God.

In the center of the page is Cerberus, the three-headed beast that guards the seat of hell, and rising up along the scale is the beast's fantastic serpentine tail, by which we come to the very throne of God. Notice the creature's three faces. When Dante is lost in a dangerous wood at the opening of *The Divine Comedy*, he is threatened by three animals. One is the lion, which represents pride, hanging on to ego, hanging on to yourself. The second is a leopard, representing lust—here it's a dog's face, desire. The third animal is a wolf, which represents fear, the past, which tears away what you've got. And so these three, they go together. This is the temptation of the Buddha. If he had hung on to his ego, lust and fear would have moved him. They didn't. Yet they're moving us, and so we're stuck.

The first of the muses—her name is Thalia—is shown under the ground. She's called "silent Thalia" because we can't hear her. As long as we're hanging on to ego, and fear, and desire—hanging on to our own personal problems—we're not hearing the voice of the universe. So, relax. I'm reminded of a picture showing the figure of Death playing the violin to the artist. Let Death talk to you and you break out of your ego pride. That means you've got to put your head in the mouth of the lion. Face the real experience of today. Don't reread it in terms of past experiences.

One of the problems addressed by Zen is that of having an experience. People talk about trying to learn the meaning of life. Life has no meaning.

What's the meaning of a flower? What we are looking for is an experience of life, getting the experience. But we're shoving ourselves off the experience by naming, translating, and classifying every experience that comes to us. You fall in love. O.K., is this going to lead to marriage or is this illicit or whatnot. You've classified and lost the experience. So, put your head in the lion's mouth and just say, "I don't know what the hell is going on." And something will come out of it.

So we put our heads into the mouth of the lion and let come what may, and we experience an artistic exaltation that rises, along Cerberus' body, through the notes of the conjoint tetrachord—what we now would call the A-minor scale. On the right are the names of the corresponding Greek musical modes, and on the left are the names of the notes of the scale in their classical form.

So through our artistic exaltation we come finally to the Apollonian radiance that moves the three graces: Euphrosyne pouring the energy down into the world; Aglaia, splendor, carrying it back; and, in the middle, Thalia—the same name as the muse— uniting the two. Remember, this is a translation of the classical, pagan, Hermetic symbology. In the recognized biblical translation these three female forms become the male persons of the Trinity: Jesus, dying in love and pouring grace into the world; the Paraclete carrying us back; and the Father, whose right and left sides are these two powers. And again, at the top, instead of simply a radiant substance, we have a personification of that substance as Apollo. So Garforius's composition is a very compact statement of the relationship of the arts to exaltations and transformations of consciousness.

Let's now return to the middle of the Pietroasa bowl, to the inner circle of figures surrounding the pivotal deity with the chalice. The reclining human being is the mind that has not experienced the initiation. It is, as it were, in sleep. It sees a dog chasing a rabbit, two gazelles eating a plant, and a lion and a leopard about to eat the gazelles. "All is sorrowful, oh dear, oh dear." But the illuminated one knows that this is a manifestation in secondary forms of the dynamic process of being.

On the ceiling of Domatilla Catacomb, we have Orpheus playing the lyre. One would have expected to see the Christ. The surrounding panels depict Old Testament, New Testament, and pagan sacrificial scenes. In other words, there was a coordination in early Christian Rome of not only the Old and New Testaments, but also the New Testament and the pagan tradition. And why not?

There was a great deal of discussion in the first four centuries whether Christianity had anything to do with Judaism. That is to say, was the Son, Jesus, the son of Yahweh, or of a higher power of which Yahweh was ignorant? Yahweh was called the fool because he didn't realize there was a higher power than himself. He thought he was God. And the son, then, who was to carry us past this, was a revelation of a higher light. And so Yahweh was associated with the demiurge who brought about all the agony and evil and sorrow in the world. This was a very definite thrust in the early Christian tradition, and it was simply a matter of fortune that the New and the Old Testaments were then united and that the New was seen as a fulfillment of the promise of the Old. That's why, when you read a Bible, you'll see a lot of footnotes in the Old Testament pointing to predictions for text in the New, and vice versa: they were woven together. Well, you could have woven early Christianity back to the Greek traditions just as well. Those traditions also existed, and why should they be separated? So, read mystically—and this is the point I would like to bring out— read mystically, all of these traditions are telling us this great, great story of our identity with the eternal power and our loss of that sense of identity when we get involved in the ego-bound world of fear and desire.

The religious tradition that was put into you in infancy is still there. There's no use getting rid of it just because you can't interpret these forms in terms of modern scientific realizations. There cannot have been an ascension to heaven. There cannot have been an assumption to heaven. There is no heaven. Even at the speed of light those bodies would not yet be out of the galaxy. But we're taught that this assumption and this ascension were physical events when they can't have been. Such an interpretation is losing the message in the symbol. The coordination of earthly and spiritual realizations can be interpreted out of those symbols.

Another aspect of Orpheus is that he was torn apart, as Jesus was torn apart in the scourging and crucifixion. What does this represent in the older, let's say, *Corpus hermeticum* way of reading it? First, that eternity is in love with the forms of time, but to come into those forms it has to be dismembered, and then, that you, as a separate entity in the form of time, in order to lose your commitment to this little instance, you must be dismembered and opened to the transcendent. So the cross, in this tradition, represents the threshold from eternity to time and from time back to eternity. And that's

also the symbology of the two trees in the Garden of Eden. The tree of knowledge of good and evil is the tree of going from unity into multiplicity, and the tree of eternal life is that of going from multiplicity to unity. It's the same tree in two directions. Some of the discussions in the rabbinical Midrash, during the first five centuries or so of the Jewish Diaspora, revolve around the question "What about the two trees in the garden?" They're seen in various aspects, but it all comes out in these two senses.

So, Orpheus comes into the world and is then torn apart. And his head is ripped off, but as it floats to Lesbos, it is still singing, singing the song of the muse.

And, finally, see what we have here: Orpheus-Bacchus crucified, from a cylinder seal of A.D. 300. There's the crucifixion as metaphysical symbol—Orpheus in the same sense as the Christ, and he goes to the cross like a bridegroom to the bride. Atop the cross is the moon—the death and resurrection motif—and above that, seven stars representing the Pleiades, known to antiquity as the Lyre of Orpheus. All you have to do is spend a little while with these things and they sing to you.

I'm going to make just a brief reference to what happened with Christianity in those early centuries. There was a conflict between two interpretations of the Christ: either as an example of the mystery hero who dies to be resurrected or as the unique incarnation. That was the big argument between the Gnostics and the Orthodox Christian community. The Orthodox community opted for the importance of the historicity of the incarnation, and to know what the Christian belief is, you have only to recite the credo known as the "Apostles' Creed" with attention to what you're saying.

"I believe in God, the Father Almighty, Creator of heaven and earth." That's that. "And in Jesus Christ, His only Son, our Lord; Who was conceived by the Holy Ghost, born of the Virgin Mary . . . suffered under Pontius Pilate, was crucified, died, and was buried." Now those last few phrases—"suffered under Pontius Pilate, was crucified, died, and was buried"—are the only historical statements in that sentence. The rest of it is mythology. "He descended into hell." This is all to be taken literally. "The third day He rose again from the dead. He ascended into heaven, sitteth at the right hand of God, the Father Almighty, from whence He shall come to judge the living and the dead." Do you believe those things literally? "I believe in the Holy Ghost, the holy Catholic church, the communion of saints, the forgiveness of sins, the resurrection of the body, and life everlasting. Amen."

Now as for the resurrection of the body, I can give you some assurance on that. You'll be thirty-five years old, the age of the body in its perfection. So, try to remember how it was back then, or get ready for a good-looking future condition, and you'll have life everlasting. Thirty-five years old, perfect—and won't it be a bore? O.K., that's the story.

in an organism. Everything is done with an enormous emphasis on ritual, rules, laws. Read the law books of the Old Testament—Leviticus, for example—and you'll see what it is.

This Near Eastern tradition was brought into Europe and applied by military force in the fourth and fifth centuries A.D., and there was enormous dislocation. By the eleventh and twelfth centuries, the ones we're talking about, Europe was beginning to assimilate this material, and the Grail story and the Arthurian romances represent that assimilation. Those were beautiful years, 1150 to 1250. Why did this flowering suddenly stop? You've all heard of the Inquisition: the College of Cardinals telling you what to think —what God thinks—and how you are supposed to relate to that instead of to this other experience—namely, of the divine power operative in your own heart. That stopped it, for the Grail romance is of the God in your own heart, and the Christ becomes a metaphor, a symbol, for that transcendent power which is the support and being of your own life. This is the understanding that we're going to get from the Grail story.

With respect to *The Quest of the Holy Grail*, it opens with the knights of Arthur's court in the great dining hall, where Arthur will not let the meal be served until an adventure has occurred. Now, in those days adventures did occur, so no one thought he was going to go away without food. The adventure, in this case, is that the Grail appears, carried by angelic messengers and covered with a veil, and it hovers above the company. Everyone sits there in rapture, and then the Grail is withdrawn. That is the call to adventure, and Gawain—a name that is going to recur a great deal—Sir Gawain, the nephew of King Arthur, stands up and says, "I propose a quest. I propose that we now should go in quest of that Grail, each to behold it unveiled."

There then occurs in the Old French text a passage that Malory, for some reason or another, did not translate, but one that seems to me to epitomize the whole sense of this Grail symbology. "They agreed that all would go on this quest, but they thought it would be a disgrace"—and that's the word used—"to go forth in a group." Think of the group psychology that the Oriental tradition represents— "they thought it would be a disgrace to go forth in a group, so each entered the forest"—the forest of the adventure—"at a point that he, himself, had chosen, where it was darkest and there was no path."

Now all of you who have had anything to do with Oriental gurus know that they have the path, and they know where you are on the path. Some of them will give you their picture to wear, so you know where you are to get to, instead of your own picture. This is the difference, and this is Europe.

So the knights entered the forest at the point that they had chosen, where there was no path. If there is a path, it is someone else's path, and you are not on the adventure. Now, what are you to do about instruction? You can get clues from people who have followed paths, but then you have to carom off that and translate it into your own decision, and there is no book of rules. On this wonderful quest —it's a marvelous romance, with each knight going his own way—when anyone finds the path of another and thinks, "Oh, he's getting there!" and begins to follow that path, then he goes astray totally, even though the other may get there. This is a wonderful story: that which we intend, that which is the journey, that which is the goal, is the fulfillment of something that never was on the earth before— namely, your own potentiality. Every thumbprint is different from every other. Every cell and structure in your body is different from that of anyone who has ever been on earth before, so you have to work it out yourself, taking your clues from here and there.

So, after we briefly review some of the historical background that underlies the tradition of the quest that the Arthurian romances illustrate, we will move into the two great stories of this tradition: that of the quest for the Grail, and the story of Tristan and Isolde.

The story of Tristan and Isolde is the story of love as the guide, love as a divine infusion. The date for the early troubadours, who were the first to celebrate this great theme, was the twelfth century—the troubadour century. The great theme was what is known as courtly love, which was by definition adulterous love.

A marriage, in the courts of those days, was a marriage arranged by the family, not a marriage of individual choice. That's the kind of marriage that predominates to this day in the East, and it was the kind of marriage of the ancient world. Two people who have never seen each other before are joined in marriage, and the church then sacramentalizes this and says, "two bodies, one flesh." What it really is is "two bank accounts, one bank account." You don't have the electrification of love at all, although you may have a very warm, genial, social relationship, production of children, and all of that sort of thing. Love entered such a situation as a destiny—a terrifying destiny, because the social response was death.

In the Gottfried von Strassburg *Tristan*, which is the Tristan that Wagner took over, there's a wonderful moment when Tristan is bringing Isolde back to Cornwall from Ireland—she was a Dublin girl—to marry his uncle, King Mark. Now Isolde's mother has sent along a nurse, Brangaene, with a love potion that is supposed to be drunk by Isolde and King Mark. But on board the ship, she leaves the potion unguarded, and the young couple, thinking it is wine, drink it.

Well, they're just a couple of kids, about fifteen years old, and they have no idea what has happened to them, and they begin to feel sick. They don't know what it is, but Isolde—apparently girls catch on to these things faster than boys—says, "L'étoile cherche la mer." She pronounces *la mer* as if it were *l'amour*, sort of in-between. Is it the sea? Are we seasick? Is this what is called love?

The whole sense of the courtly idea was the pain of love. Unless you've got it in the gut and can hardly bear it, it hasn't happened. The idea was to feel; the Buddha says all life is sorrowful. This is the experience of the pain of being alive. Where your pain is, that's where your life is. So find it.

When Brangaene realizes what has happened, she's appalled. She goes to Tristan and says, "Tristan, you have drunk your death." Then there's this wonderful line in the Gottfried version. Tristan says, "I don't know what you mean. If by death you mean the pain of my love for Isolde, that's my life. If by death you mean the punishment that I am to suffer from society, I accept that. If by death you mean eternal damnation in hell, I accept that." Now there's the individual experience —refuting the values of the whole system. That's what these people represent. We're dealing with something serious here.

So after our historical review, I want to talk about the Tristan problem, which leaves a tension between the social order—which is imported, implanted, and put on the person—and the individual life. They don't go together. The word *amor*, Provençal for *amour*, spelled backwards is *roma*. So *roma* is the Roman Catholic church and its sacraments, and *amor* is individual experience. By what kind of magic can people put God in your heart? They can't. He's either there or not there, out of your own experience. That's the sense of this thing. Consequently, when we come to the Grail of Wolfram von Eschenbach, there is the problem of coordinating these two.

The theme of the Grail is the bringing of life into what is known as "the waste land." The waste land is the preliminary theme to which the Grail is the answer. What is the sense of "the waste land" in medieval terms and in T. S. Eliot's terms in his key poem, *The Waste Land*? It's exactly the same sense. It's the world of people living inauthentic lives—doing what they're supposed to do. In the twelfth century, people had to profess beliefs that they may or may not have held, they had to love in marriage people that they may or may not have learned to love, and they had to behave the way that the cardinals told them to behave. And as you will see when Parzival fails in the Grail adventure, he fails because he's doing what he's been told to do instead of what his heart tells him to do.

I want now to give some sense of the fantastic traditions and the levels of culture that have piled up in Europe, which is not the youngest but the oldest culture in the world—going way back to the caves. Lascaux and the other caves date from 30,000 B.C., and there's nothing like them on the planet for many, many millennia afterwards. Then on top of that tradition comes the Neolithic, the tradition of the early planting people. Then come the great Bronze Age traditions, then come the invading Indo-European warrior traditions, then comes the Roman tradition, then come the Christian traditions—each one piled right on top of the other. So I want to give a view of that development, and then we'll move into the two great stories: first Tristan, and then the Grail.

Merlin was the great "guru" of the Arthurian world. He had the whole program in his mind. The world of the Arthurian knights was a world of two great stages or periods. The first was that of Christianizing—or civilizing, you might say—the wild Iron Age, the barbaric world of Europe. After that came the age of the individual journey, the individual adventure. Now Merlin is a purely fictional figure, who's associated with the Druid mysteries. He's a sort of late manifestation of the Druid tradition. The Druids were the priests and spiritual guardians of the Celts, who came into Europe from Bavaria during the first millennium B.C. in two stages. The first stage, known as the Hallstatt culture, was what might be called an "oxcart" culture: slow waves of herding people with their families in ox-drawn carts lumbering into the European wilderness and domesticating it. The second stage of invasion, beginning around 500 B.C., was during the period known as La Tène culture, which was centered in southern France and Switzerland. It was then that brilliant chariot warriors came in and went up into the British Isles.

The people who had been living in Europe before these invasions were pre-Celtic, pre–Indo-European, and

their tradition may go back all the way to the caves. But the great period of their flowering was that of Stonehenge. Since Stonehenge was built in three or four different stages, its dates range from 1800 to 1400 B.C. In the medieval tradition Merlin is supposed to have brought the stones to Stonehenge.

There is an arch in Algeria, from the same period, and you recognize this from Mycenae. The way the uprights and the cross-beams are put together is exactly the way they're put together at Stonehenge. So, Stonehenge, or at least the great sarsen ring of Stonehenge, is of approximately the same date as Mycenae, the middle of the second millennium B.C., which is also the period of the High Bronze Age and

not only in this zone but in other zones as well. The people from an arid, relatively desert land come into a rich river valley land as conquerors. They're sturdy people. They've had a tough time. They impose themselves on the area, but they absorb the civilization from below, and the people below absorb their language and mythology, and you get this marriage. The same thing is happening at the same time in the Near East, where you have the Semites coming in. Again we have two groups—the people of the land and the people of the desert who come in as conquerors.

The Celts were just one group of Indo-Europeans. The first group of them come in, about 1000 B.C., as a lumbering, heavily laden people with their herds and families. Then in Switzerland and southern France, we have a new development, La Tène culture, great vigorous warrior tribes.

This is the Gringastip bowl from Denmark. We begin to have a notion

of the deities of these people. The deer sheds its antlers and the antlers grow again. Any animal that has this kind of cycle becomes associated with the cosmic cycle, and the deer becomes a very important symbolic animal here. Any deity that may show itself as an animal can also show itself as a human being. If you have a real mythological tradition, the emphasis is not on the form of the god, but on the energy of the god. That energy can show itself in an animal form, in a human form, in the form of a rock—all kinds of forms. Here is the serpent that sheds its skin to be born again, and here is what is known as a torque, a neckpiece. Gold is the color of the sun. The serpent is the animal of the moon. We have here the solar torque of gold and the serpent that sheds its skin. The deity represents the synthesis of those two worlds. You get this same symbolic theme in Kundalini yoga, where the two nerves, *idā* and *pingalā*, represent lunar and solar. So this is Cernunnos, one of the deities of the Celts.

To review, we have the old European Bronze Age culture, and on top of that we have the Celtic warrior traditions, and now the Romans come in (Caesar's *Gallic Wars*, 50 B.C.), and we have the Roman overlay.

This is a monument from the Roman period, probably dating between the first century B.C. and the first A.D. This figure has the antlers of a deer—the same god that we've just seen. In his lap is a cornucopia, and from it pours, inexhaustibly, the food. This is the Grail, the vessel of inexhaustible vitality. The Grail is that fountain in the center of the universe from which the energies of eternity pour into the

world of time. It's in each of our hearts, that same energy. The grain comes out, and a deer and a bull feed. The deer is the wild animal, the bull is the domestic animal, symbolic of the lunar life. The two deities are Roman deities—Apollo and Mercury. Caesar, in the sixth chapter of his *Gallic Wars*, describes the gods of the Celts but gives them Roman names. This is wonderful: the Romans, and before them the Greeks, could see that the gods of other people were the same gods they worshiped, because those gods are personifications of the energies that shape and maintain the universe. So Caesar could go into Gaul and say, "He whom you call Cernunnos we call Pluto." When Alexander the Great went into India, 327 B.C., he recognized Krishna as a counterpart of Herakles and Indra as a counterpart of Zeus. So there no missionizing, but rather a wonderful recognition. But you could not possibly say, "He whom you call Ashur we call Yahweh." And why is that? That's because for the Celtic tribes, the desert people, the principal divinities were the tribal gods, the patrons of their tribes, and the gods of nature were secondary or nonexistent. But in the Greek and Roman traditions, the principal deities are the deities that support the universe and the secondary deity is the tribal patron—the one who happens to be the guardian and advisor of a particular race. These two mythological perspectives are in total contrast. One is exclusive, the other is what is called syncretic. So, with the Romans we begin to have a combination of classical and Celtic divinities, and they all come from the same Indo-European Bronze Age background. There's a wonderful coordination taking place.

The Roman Empire was vast and included the whole world of the Near East, North Africa, and Europe. Alexander had gone through to India. King Ashoka, the great Buddhist king of the third century B.C., had sent Buddhist missionaries to Cyprus, to Macedon, and to Alexandria. So Hinduism and the Gnosticism of Buddhism were also operating in the Roman Empire and underlying these symbols, and these people knew about it. The Roman army included a lot of Persians who were sent up to Britain to defend the borders. The Danube was another border, and the Roman armies along there included many soldiers from the Orient. Then, in the fifth century, the Huns from Asia come smashing in with Attila, and they hit the Ostrogoths, who then bump into the Visigoths, and they in turn run into the Sarmatians, and so forth and so on, and the Roman lines cannot hold. Rome collapses.

Now I want to turn to something

from this period that was found in the Pyrenees and is a big surprise. Just to the west of Lourdes is a little place called St. Pé, where we have this monument from the first century A.D. And what it says is "Lexiia, the daughter of Odan, has gained merit through her vows to Artehe." This shows us that already in the period of Roman Europe, Arthur, Artehe, was revered as a god. He's originally a Celtic god, and the place where we find him revered is in the Pyrenees. The name Artus, Arthur, is related to Artemis, Arcturus, and all of these are related to the deity, the bear. The bear is the oldest worshiped deity in the world. And in this part of the world, we have bear shrines going back to Neanderthal times, perhaps 100,000 B.C.

So much for the Roman Empire up to the fourth century. Then we have Constantine, who converts that whole empire into a Christian empire. Along the Danube, as I said, there were Persian soldiers, and the Persian myth at that time was of Mithra. Mithra's great sacrifice was to kill the bull—the original cosmic bull—which releases the energies of life to the world. The sacrifice is the sacrifice of the container of the energy for the release of the energy. The contrast between the Mithraic and Christian religions, which were contemporary rivals for the Roman mind, was that in the Christian tradition the savior is the one who is killed, while in the Mithraic, the savior is the one who kills. Actually, the one killed and the one doing the killing— this is the same power.

This is why the Christian tradition has done a mean job on Judas. He is the midwife of our salvation. The negative and the positive are two aspects of the play in the field of time of the one power. According to the Gospels, at the Last Supper Jesus says, "He to whom I give the sop will betray me." He then dips a piece of bread in the wine and hands it to Judas. Is that not an assignment? Of the twelve, Judas is the one worthy to play the counter role to the sacrifice.

After Constantine, in the latter half of the fourth century, comes Theodo-sius, who declares that "no religion is to exist in the Roman Empire but the Christian religion, no form of the Christian religion but that of the Byzantine throne." So then starts an exodus to the Orient of Roman, Syrian, and other artists, and there is a great new flowering of the Persian and Indian arts and a complete collapse of the European. This is the fourth and fifth centuries. When did Europe come back? In the period we're talking about, and this is quite a story. A map showing the extent of the Christian empire—the Christianization of Europe—includes England and, specifically, Ireland, converted by Saint Patrick in the fifth century. And now what happens? Along the Danube are the German tribes. Bang! Rome collapses. The invasions take place. And now comes the invasion we're interested in. The Romans had to pull out of England around A.D. 450 to shorten their lines. They couldn't maintain themselves. That left England naked, like an oyster with the shell removed. There was no defense. And it was then that the Anglo-Saxons—the Danes, the Frisians, the people from Denmark and Germany—came pouring in.

This is the period of the warrior Arthur. The earlier god was down in the Pyrenees. Now we come to the fourth and fifth centuries A.D. in Britain, and there is a man named Arthur who fights for the Britains—that is to say, the Celtic people—against the invading English. This particular Arthur was not a king. The chroniclers of the time, Gildas (d. 570) and Nennius (fl. ca. 800), speak of him as a *dux bellorum,* a leader in war. He was a military man, a native fighter trained by the Romans, and he assisted the native British kings in their battles. To him are assigned, two or three centuries after his death, great victories in twelve battles. Twelve? You've got the zodiac. You've got a Sun King. He's already being identified with the gods. So this Artus Dux Bellorum becomes synthesized with the god image in the popular talk.

The British lost. The English won, but they won only in the area that the Romans had held. They did not go into Cornwall. They did not conquer Wales. They did not go into Scotland. So the old Celtic tradition survives in Ireland and in Wales and in Scotland. I would call this the Celtic matrix. All kinds of Celtic stories survive there.

The people from the south of England, the Bretons, immigrated to Brittany, and a legend grew up among them. Arthur was the great defender. He will return. He will restore us to our mother land. This is known as the Hope of the Bretons, and it's out of Brittany that much of this Arthurian legendry comes—refreshed, in the oral tradition, by material from Ireland and Wales—so there's a lot of old Celtic stuff associated with the stories.

What has been going on meanwhile? In the seventh century A.D. there was a whole new problem—the rise of Islam. The Christians had been arguing about the relationship of the Son to the Father and the Holy Ghost to the Father and the Son, and all this kind of business. Then Muhammad comes along and says, "There's no God but God, and Muhammad is His Prophet." And what a relief that was. So with all the philosophical and theological arguments annihilated with just the statement "There's no God but God," Islam swept through much of the former Roman Empire and, within one century, the Moors were into Spain and at the gates of India.

Then, in A.D. 800, Charles the Great, Charlemagne, united Europe in the Christian empire, but when you read European history you wonder how the place survived at all. So we've had the German invasions, and then the Muslims sweeping across southern Europe, and now we have the Norse, the Vikings—riding up the rivers of Europe, burning cities. This was the period—the eighth, ninth, and tenth centuries—when in the Litany was the prayer "From the fury of the Normans, O Lord, deliver us." They were a wild, ferocious people who intentionally inspired terror. The imperiled

Christian world had three hundred years of this kind of thing and was really in trouble.

Ireland had not been invaded by the Germanic people and was a stand of the old Christian traditions. Nonetheless, towers of refuge were built throughout Ireland during the ninth century. Here is a tenth-century stone cross from northeast Ireland. On its side is a symbolic design that suggests Chakras 4, 5, 6, and 7 of the Kundalini and the two serpents of *idā* and *pingalā*. So underlying this tradition that we're talking about are these esoteric traditions.

The empire of Charlemagne survives the turmoil and then is split into three domains for his three sons. To one, he gave the world which is now France. To the second, he gave Germany, and to the third, Alsace-Lorraine, which has been back and forth between the two ever since.

An interesting thing then begins to happen: modern language evolves— French out of Latin, and German out of the Old Germanic. Whereas in Latin, the subject and the verb are together—*amo*, I love; *amas*, thou lovest; and so forth—now the subject begins to break away from the verb. Here again is the emphasis on the individual: *ich liebe*, I love.

In 1066 we have a new conquest of the British Isles, this time by William the Conqueror. In 1097 Pope Urban preaches the first crusade, and Europe, which has been squabbling, is united in one cause—going to the Near East to save the shrines of the Holy Land from the Muslims. So by the eleventh and twelfth centuries, the life of every young man had to be that of a warrior, of a knight, of a fighter. And when war is the career, war games are the play. So you have this whole tradition of jousting and of battle: with their ladies watching, the young men show off, knock each other off their horses, and go into battle, each for his lady, wearing her scarf in his helmet.

There's a wonderful story of Guinevere and Lancelot, her lover. She wants to show her power, so she tells him to go into the jousting as a fool. "Lose, don't win," she says. "Get knocked off your horse until I give you a sign, and then let go." So Lancelot, a knight who always does what his lady wants, goes into the joust, gets knocked around, and then, at a signal from Guinevere, defeats his opponents.

This is the background of Tristan and the Grail. We have this great esoteric information in the images, with what appears to be just superficial play going on.

12

A Noble Heart:
The Courtly Love of
Tristan and Isolde

Geoffrey of Monmouth's *History of the Kings of Britain* is our first account of Arthur as a king. We now know from the Chronicles that he was not a king but a *dux bellorum,* a war leader, who assisted the British kings in defending the land against the in-

coming Anglo-Saxons and Jutes. He died, and the land was conquered— at least what we now call England was conquered. The Celtic lands and the earlier Celtic people were not— the Scots, the Welsh, the Cornish, the Irish, and the people of the Isle of Man. Well, that's a treasure trove, you might say, of the old Celtic traditions. It's out of there and Brittany that this material comes.

Then we have the conquest of the English who have conquered the Celts. The conquest of the English in

1066—the only date that most people know—by William the Conqueror brings the north French, really the Norman people, into Britain.

The situation was much as it is on a college campus. The freshmen have been persecuted by the sophomores. The Celts have been persecuted by the English. Next year they all move up. In comes another freshman class. This earlier freshman class is now the sophomore class, and they're doing the persecuting. But this sophomore class was formerly the freshman class that was persecuted by the sophomores who are now the juniors. So there's a kind of fellowship between the juniors and the freshmen against the sophomores. Accordingly, the Celts (the juniors) and the Normans (the freshmen) are against the English (the sophomores).

The English were put out into the pigsties and nobody spoke English in England. They all spoke Norman French. To this day, we use Norman French words for the meat that appears on the table and English words for the meat that is out on the farm. Swine out there, pork at the table. Calves out there, veal at the table.

These Normans didn't have TV, so what did they do with their time? Well, they liked to hear stories, and the old Celtic tales are some of the best stories in the world. So this whole tra- dition of oral bardic literature that has grown up—"The Hope of the Bret- ons" and so forth—is recounted in the Norman courts by the bards.

Meanwhile, there's this great, great dame of the whole Middle Ages: Eleanor of Aquitaine. She was the wife of two great kings. She was married to King Louis of France, went with him on the Crusades, and came back com- pletely bored with Louis. So one morning he wakes up and discovers that Eleanor has gone to marry the fu- ture king of England, Henry II. So she's the wife of two kings, she's the mother of King Richard the Lion-Heart and of King John, and she's the grand- mother of every royal head in the land of Europe in the next generation. She's it. Her period is exactly the period of the Grail romances.

Now where did Eleanor of Aqui- taine come from? She came from the south of France. So she brings the south of France to the English throne and is the inheritor of the traditions of the whole of Europe. Her grandfather, William of Poitiers, was the first of the troubadours. Now the Arthurian tra- dition, through the bards, goes to the Continent. But the Continent isn't in- terested in Arthur, it's interested in his knights—the stories of these Celtic heroes transformed into Christian, armor-clad knights. Meanwhile, the stories come into the field of courtly love. Eleanor, her granddaughter Blanche of Castile, and her daughter Marie of Champagne were the great ladies of the period. They were the ones who were the cultivators of the whole theme of courtly love.

And as I've said already, courtly love had to do with love and not with marriage. The whole tradition of the troubadours has to do with love, and our tradition of psychology begins at that time. What is the psychology of love? What happens when this thing strikes? There were debates among the troubadours as to what love was. One of the most apt formulations was that of the troubadour Girhault de Borneilh: "The eyes are the scouts of the heart. The eyes go forth to find an image to recommend to the heart. And when the eyes have found such an image, if the heart [and here's the key word] is a gentle heart [that means a heart capable not simply of lust but of love, two totally different things] then love is born." This is news.

When you hear talk about love from pulpits, there are two kinds of love, and neither one is personal. The first kind of love is lust, which I define as the zeal of the organs for each other. It's completely impersonal. The other kind of love is agape, spiritual love—"love thy neighbor as thyself"—no matter who it is. It, too, is completely impersonal. Now here comes Europe,

the personal experience: "The eyes go forth to find an image to recommend to the heart." This is not a heart of lust, but a heart that knows how to respond to an image. That's the rescue—delight in the manifestation of the divine in a person. When the heart is completely taken by this image of love, nothing else counts; and in the courtly tradition, nothing else counted. *Amour.* And what is the principal threat? Honor. So you find in these traditions of the Middle Ages this conflict between honor and love. The ultimate sacrifice for a noble heart is the sacrifice of honor for love. So that's the theme that we're up against here.

There are a lot of wonderful stories about the troubadours. There's an entire volume from the twelfth century on the lives of the troubadours and their wild absurdities to win the woman's regard. One troubadour falls in love with a woman whose name means wolf. He clothes himself in a wolf skin and pretends, as a wolf, to attack a flock of sheep. Of course the sheep dogs pounce on him and tear him to pieces and he's in pretty bad shape, so he's taken into the woman's castle to be healed—by her and her husband. Another buys himself the robe of a leper and cuts off two of his fingers and then sits among the lepers. The lady comes out of her castle and says, "Well, my God, there's Gerard."

So he wins her regard that way. These troubadour stories are wonderful.

Then there were the courts of love, where the ladies sat in judgment on cases. For example, there's one very famous case of a gentleman who proposes himself to a lady as her lover, but she says, "No. I have a lover. But if I cast him off or lose him, then you're next in line." Well, her husband dies, she marries her lover, and along comes Buddy, who says, "Here I am." She says, "Why no, I've married my lover." He says, "Well, you know there is no such thing as married love." So he brought it to the court, which declared that married love is a contradiction in terms and that he was next in line. So you have this tension in the medieval world between these two traditions.

The principal language for the celebration of courtly love was Provençal, or langue d'oc, the language of the south of France. I spent a whole year working on langue d'oc at the University of Paris, and it's pretty boring stuff. But the interest is formal; for example, how to get the lady's name into the poem without her husband recognizing it. So a lot of the intricacies of poetic virtuosity have to do with this hidden address to the lady.

An important thing about courtly love is that the lady must assure herself that the suitor is a gentle heart and not just a lusty boy. So you have this whole tradition of delay, and test, and trial. If the chap is good with a sword and a lance, he's sent out to guard a bridge. Traffic in the Middle Ages was considerably encumbered by young men guarding bridges who wouldn't let anybody across. Or if he's better with the pen than with the sword, he's told to write poems, things like that. When the lady is assured that what is being addressed to her is the gentle and not the lusty heart, she may grant what is known as *merci*. That's a technical term. Now *merci*, and the degree of *merci* that's granted, will depend on the lady's opinion of the lover. It may consist in the privilege of kissing her on the back of the neck once every Whitsuntide, or it may go considerably further than that. The lady who accepts service without, at some time, ultimately expressing either *merci* or rejection is *sauvage*, "savage." In one medieval story of a woman who was *sauvage*, her suitor, trying to prove himself in battle, disports in a wild way and gets killed. Then she realizes.

So the Arthurian romances, the stories of the knights, appear on the Continent. The first writer was Chrétien de Troyes, the court poet of Marie of Champagne. Chrétien began writing at the end of the twelfth century—

Well, Guinevere kept being abducted, and this time she's abducted by the lord of a castle which is equated with the underworld. Arthur doesn't go to get her back; Lancelot goes. And he goes with such speed that he rides two horses to death. Well, after you've lost two horses, and you don't have another, and here you are walking in a suit of armor, you're not getting very far very fast. He's plowing along there, and a cart, driven by a churl, a peasant, passes him. In the cart are people who are being taken to be hanged or punished in one way or another. And he thinks, "If I were in that cart I'd get faster to Guinevere's rescue. But then, this would be a loss of honor to my armor, and my role as knight." So he hesitates for three steps before getting into the cart. But he does get in, and an adventure begins.

Well, the adventure includes a couple of trials, one of which is my favorite for the whole Middle Ages—the Trial of the Perilous Bed. A number of knights have to experience the Perilous Bed. You come into a room that's absolutely empty, except in the middle of it is a bed on rollers. You are to come in dressed in your full armor—sword, spear, shield, all that heavy stuff—and get into that bed. Well, as the knight approaches the bed, it shears away to one side. So he comes again, and it goes the other way. The knight finally thinks, "I've got to jump." So with his full gear, he jumps into the bed, and as soon as he hits the bed, it starts bucking like a bronco all over the room, banging against the walls and all that kind of thing, and then it stops. Then he's told, "It's not finished yet. Keep your armor on and keep your shield over yourself." And then arrows and crossbow bolts pummel him—bang, bang, bang, bang. Then a lion appears and attacks the knight, but he cuts off the lion's feet, and the two of them end up lying there in a pool of blood.

Then the ladies of the castle that's to be disenchanted by this great event come in and see their knight, their savior, lying there looking dead. One of them takes a bit of fur from her garment and puts it in front of his nose and it moves ever so slightly—he's breathing, he's alive. So, they nurse him back to health, and the castle is disenchanted. Lancelot went through this.

My great friend Heinrich Zimmer, talking about these materials, one time asked, "What's the meaning of a trial of this kind?" This is what you must do if you're going to interpret symbols. You've got to figure out the meaning of a thing like this. His answer, and I think it's probably correct, is that this is the masculine experience of the feminine temperament: it doesn't quite make sense, but there it is. That's the way it's going this time, that's the way it's going that. And he said, "The trial is to hold on." Be patient and don't try to solve it. Just endure it, and then all the boons of beautiful womanhood will be yours.

Well, the next trial of our friend Lancelot is what is known as the Sword Bridge. This is a bridge, made of a sword, across a roaring torrent. Lancelot has to go across with bare hands and feet on the sharp edge of the sword. Perhaps you know Somerset Maugham's novel entitled *The Razor's Edge*. This is a motif from the Kana Upanishad. "Any trip along your own path is a razor's edge." It really is; nobody's done it before. And it's so easy —particularly if what you're following is your bliss, your passion—it's so easy to tip over and fall into a torrent of passion that sweeps you away. This is a real lesson. So, having survived the Perilous Bed, Lancelot survives the Sword Bridge, and then he has disenchanted the castle in which Guinevere is a captive. He comes in to receive her great greeting and gratitude. But she's as cold as ice. Why? Because he hesitated for three steps before getting in that cart. How did she know? She's the goddess: women know these things. So that's the beautiful story of Lancelot, and it's the great one, Chrétien's best.

His next story, *Yvain*, is one that appears also in a Welsh version, known as the Lady of the Fountain. I won't go through the whole story, just a bare outline. A knight comes to Arthur's court and tells of an adventure in which he has failed. There was a castle, a tree, a spring under the tree, a stone beside the spring, a ladle hanging from the tree, and the adventure consisted in dipping water from the spring onto the stone, at which moment a terrific storm arose, all the leaves and birds were blown from the tree, and out of the castle came storming the Black Knight—the thunder knight—who engaged in combat with the one that had dipped the water and overthrew him. Well, Sir Yvain, on hearing this story, says he's going to attempt the adventure. And he does. And when the knight comes out, Yvain runs his lance through the knight's body. The dying knight turns and, riding his horse still, gallops into the castle. Yvain follows, but gets caught with his horse between the portcullisses, the heavy castle gates that drop down. A beautiful young girl in the castle, the queen's serving maid, sees him thus caught and thinks, "This is a beautiful knight. He should become the husband of my lady who has just lost her husband." This is Frazer's story of *The Golden Bough*, where the one that kills the priest becomes

the priest of the queen. It's a hangover of an old, old mythological theme.

Yvain does become her spouse. He forgets Arthur's court, and you know what this is: you have found your bliss, but it has disengaged you from your world of duties. So he's there with her, and Arthur's knights come and pour water on the stone. He has to come out then as the Thunder Knight, and he engages in combat with Gawain. Neither one can defeat the other, and neither one knows who the other is. Then they unhelmet themselves, and Gawain says, "Oh, hi, Yvain. Come on back to the court." So then he goes with Arthur's knights to the court and forgets the lady.

This is a basic spiritual problem: the split between the two worlds. The lady then sends a messenger and tells him, "You have lost me." Yvain then tries the adventure of getting back to her. The whole story is about the ordeal of recovering the relationship to your true being and then bringing her to the court. It's the whole problem of life. It's right there in that story. Do you understand? That's the problem.

So to review: Chrétien wrote a Tristan that's been lost, and then *Érec*, *Cligès*, *Lancelot*, *Yvain*, and then he writes *Perceval*, which is his Grail story. But before I speak about Parzival, I first want to recount the Tristan story and bring out the main points there.

There were about six or eight Tristans in the Middle Ages. The most important one is that of Gottfried von Strassburg, who died before he finished it, so one has to turn to the story on which he was modeling his own. The characteristic of medieval storytelling is that you don't invent the story, you develop it. You take a traditional story and interpret it—give it new depth and meaning in terms of the conditions of your particular day. Now, the story of Tristan is of a youth whose parents have died. A typical epic hero is an orphan or the son of a widow. Tristan's mother's brother is King Mark of Cornwall. Tristan is born in Brittany. So here we have Brittany and Cornwall, the whole Celtic world. Tristan goes to his uncle's castle in Cornwall and arrives just at the time that an emissary, Morold, has come from the court of Ireland in Dublin. The Irish king has conquered the Cornish king, and he requires that every four or five years young boys and girls be sent to serve at the Irish court. This is based on the Cretan story of Theseus and the Minotaur. Morold has come to collect the youths and maidens.

The queen of Ireland, Isolt, is Isolde's mother. She has prepared a poison and put it on the sword of Morold. Tristan says to his uncle, "Let me handle that guy." His uncle says, "This is very dangerous." Tristan says, "No, this is the only way." So a jousting, a champion's battle, is prepared between Morold and Tristan.

Tristan rides against Morold. Morold's sword comes down on his knee, cuts him, the poison is injected, he's as good as dead. He replies by bringing his sword down on Morold's head, and splitting his helmet, and a piece of Tristan's sword remains in Morold's skull.

When Morold's body is brought back to Ireland, his niece, Isolde, who loved her uncle, takes the piece of Tristan's sword from his head and puts it in her little treasure chest—to remember Uncle Morold.

Meanwhile, Tristan becomes terribly sick. The wound is festering, and gangrene sets in. He says to his uncle, "Just put me in a little boat with my harp, and the boat will carry me to the source of this poison." And indeed, by magic the boat carries him to Dublin Bay. People hear this beautiful music —he was a miraculous young man— and they bring him to Queen Isolt to be cured. Since Tristan has disguised himself and calls himself Tantrist, Isolt does not recognize this chap nor realize that it is her poison that is killing him, and she cures him.

When the wound has healed to such an extent that the stench of his presence can be tolerated, she invites her daughter, Isolde, in to hear him play the harp. He plays wonderfully, and immediately the two fall in love, only they don't know it. This is the whole understanding of this story by Gottfried. They are crazy in love with each other, but they just don't know it. Tristan plays the harp better than he's ever played it in his life, and he becomes Isolde's harp teacher.

The model for this was the story of Abélard and Héloïse, which dates from 1116, one century earlier. Abélard was Héloïse's teacher and seduced her. Tristan is the teacher of Isolde.

Now this silly boy, when he's cured, goes back to Cornwall and says, "Oh, Uncle Mark, I met the most wonderful girl. She'd be just the wife for you." He speaks so gloriously of this wonderful girl that his uncle and the barons say, "Well, why don't you go over and fetch her?" So Tristan, calling himself Tantrist again, goes back to fetch Isolde for his Uncle Mark.

Do you see the courtly love problem here? Tristan has fallen in love. His uncle has never seen Isolde. Mark and Isolde's marriage is standard medieval violence. There's no love in it. So from the point of view of the courtly love, Mark is disqualified. He's simply what is technically called *le jaloux*, "the jealous one"—that's the husband.

So Tristan goes back to fetch Isolde. Well, what has happened is that a great dragon has begun to trouble the country, and the king has said, "The person who kills that dragon can have Isolde as his wife." That's good old standard medieval stuff again. The dragon's a little bit unusual, but not in stories. Meanwhile, there is a young seneschal, or courtier, who wants Isolde, but doesn't have the guts to kill the dragon. But he keeps hanging around. When anyone is going to kill the dragon, he wants to be there. Perhaps he can make the claim. So, Tristan rides at the dragon.

Now Gottfried was a cleric, a low-level priest, not a noble or a warrior, and he describes the killing of the dragon in the most amusing, comical way: the dragon bites off the first half of the horse—that kind of thing. Anyway, Tristan kills the dragon with his lance, the dragon expires, and Tristan, to stake his claim, cuts out the dragon's tongue and puts it in his shirt. Now that's the worst thing you can do with a dragon's tongue, because it's poisonous.

So Tristan is walking along with the dragon's tongue inside his shirt, and it overtakes him, and he falls into a pool. There he is, under the water, and all that's sticking out is his nose. The other chap, meanwhile, cuts off the dragon's head and presents it as his claim for Isolde.

Well, Isolde and her mother are out walking and they come past this pool, and they look down. "Why, look at that! There's a nose, and then under that a man!" So, they take Tristan out, and, since Queen Isolt is used to curing people, they take him home to cure him. His sword and his armor are with him.

Soon Tristan is recovering pretty well, and one fine day, when he's in the bathtub, Isolde is fooling around with his armor. She pulls the sword out of the sheath and Wow! There's a nick in the sword. She runs to her little treasure chest and gets the piece of sword that came out of Uncle Morold's head. It fits. So, with the sword in her hand, she goes to Tristan, who's still in the bathtub, and raises the sword to strike him. But he says, "Hold on. You kill me, and that other guy gets you." Well, the sword was getting kind of heavy anyhow, so she let that one go.

When Tristan's finally cured, there comes this wonderful affair of the giving of Isolde to the killer of the dragon. The lout comes in with the dragon's head, and Tristan just says, "Let's open the mouth and see what's inside. There's no tongue. Where's the tongue? Well, right here."

So Tristan gets the girl, but instead of taking her for himself, he's going to take her back to King Mark. So you can see what a silly boy he is. He's only fifteen years old, so he doesn't know what's actually happened to him.

Isolde's mother then prepares a love potion, but there's a secret here. The poison and the love potion are essentially the same potion—the pain of love, the sickness unto death that no doctors can cure, all that sort of thing. So the woman who brought him there by poisoning him is now preparing the love potion that's going to be the fulfillment of this whole affair. Next comes the sequence we previously re-counted: Brangaene, little Isolde's nurse, is instructed to go with them, keep the love potion, and present it to Mark and Isolde at the time of their marriage; but on the boat to Cornwall, she is careless, and Tristan and Isolde drink the potion.

Now comes a problem, a theological problem. If the love potion compels you to love, then the love of Tristan and Isolde, although it is adulterous, is not a mortal sin. To commit a mortal sin you must have a serious matter, sufficient reflection, and full consent of the will. If it's magic that's done it, there's no consent of the will, and it's a perfectly innocent love. Let's think about that. To resolve this problem, several of the authors of the Tristan story fixed it up so that the love potion would work for two or three years, and then, when it stops, sin begins.

So the couple drink the potion, and here's the situation I spoke of earlier: you have drunk your death. It's a great heroic statement in the Middle Ages. "I accept hellfire for this, and it won't be hell if I am burning with the love for Isolde." That's what it's saying. So, comes the wedding. The nastiest bit in the whole story is that Isolde, who can't bear the idea of being with Mark, persuades Brangaene to take her place in bed for the marriage night. Brangaene plays the role, and King Mark thinks it's Isolde. Now he's doubly

240

disqualified. This is inattention to details, which just eliminates him.

So Tristan and Isolde are having their affair, and King Mark presently becomes aware of it. Properly, they should be killed, but he can't bear it. He loves them both. This is a noble man. And this is a beautiful, beautiful handling of the problem: he just says, "Get out of my sight. Go away." And they go into the forest.

What follows are the forest years of Tristan and Isolde. They come to a cave, a cave fashioned by the giants of pre-Christian times—we're back to the old Celtic Germanic time—and over the entrance is an inscription, "A Chapel for Lovers." They go in, and the whole chapel is symbolic. Every detail of it has symbolic meaning—chastity, loyalty, purity, all this kind of thing. All these terms have new meanings, of course, in this context. Where the altar would have been, there is a bed of crystal, and the sacrament of this altar is the sacrament of sex. Gottfried von Strassburg meant this, and the medieval people meant this. The sacrament of love is sexual intercourse. And it is a sacrament.

Well, they're in the bed, and it's beautiful, and directly above are two

241

openings in the roof through which light comes. One fine day, they hear off in the woods the sound of hunting horns, the hunting horns of King Mark. Tristan thinks, "If King Mark comes and looks down through those openings and sees us asleep together, this will be too bad." So what does he do? He places his sword between himself and Isolde. Do you catch the sense of this? Honor against love? This is the sin of Tristan: to have put the sword between.

When Mark looks down, indeed he does see the two, with the sword between them, and he says, "Oh, I have misunderstood them." So he invites them back to court, and that, supposedly, is the end of their affair. Of course, they continue the affair, they are caught again, and this time there's no fooling. Tristan is exiled to Brittany, but before he goes, Isolde has to undergo an ordeal, which may have been an actual ordeal in the Middle Ages. She has to take an oath that she has not lain with any man but her husband. Having taken that oath, she is to take in her hand a red-hot iron bar. If her hand is not burned, she is vindicated and cleared of the accusation.

On the way to this trial, Isolde has to cross a river in a boat. So Tristan, in disguise, arranges to take the job of the boatman. So he's the ferryman who ferries her across the river, and when he has to lift her out of the boat, he manages to trip and fall on top of her.

Then she goes to the trial, where she says, "I've lain with no man but my husband and the boatman that fell on top of me." She didn't tell a lie, and the iron bar didn't burn her hand. Gottfried says, "And so you see, Christ is like a weather vane; he goes where the wind blows." That may be why Gottfried didn't finish the book. No one knows how he died, but they were burning people to death in those days for statements of that kind.

Anyhow, Tristan goes to Brittany, and now comes the last part of the story. In Brittany, he hears of a young lady whose name is Isolde. She is known as Isolde of the White Hands. And this is the kind of thing that happens in medieval romance: he falls in love with the name, and so he marries the lady, poor little Isolde of the White Hands. But because she isn't *the* Isolde, he can't have intercourse with her, he can't bring himself to that act.

So she's out riding with her brother one day and the horse steps into a puddle and the water splashes up high on her thigh and she says to her brother, "The horse is bolder than Tristan." And her brother says, "What?" She explains, and he goes to Tristan and complains. But when Tristan tells him of his love for the other

Isolde, he understands the whole thing.

Tristan then gets into a battle and is wounded unto death. The only person who could cure him would be the Isolde that he loves, so he sends his wife's brother to bring her to him. They have an arrangement: if Isolde has consented to come, the boat will have a white sail; if she has refused, it will have a black sail. So he's dying in his wife's arms, the boat is coming, and she tells him the sail is black—actually it's white—and he dies. There's the Tristan story. There are echoes of Theseus and the Minotaur throughout it.

So the situation is love against marriage, and you might call it the counterculture against the culture. Marriages in medieval Europe were customarily arranged by the families, the aristocracy regarded this as intolerable, and so there was a celebration of the theme of love. How do we bring these things together?

I want now to give you the Grail answer, which is, in my thinking, one of the great, great stories of the Middle Ages. I think Wolfram von Eschenbach's *Parzival* is *the* high story of the Middle Ages. I would put it above Dante's *Divine Comedy*, for Dante ends up in heaven, while Gottfried ends up on earth, and the thing is solved here, now, in the flesh, and in a magnificent way.

telle maniere que nulz deulz nauoit pou
oir de parler ains se regardoient aussi
comme cilz fussent tous bestes mues.
Lors entre leans le saint graal couuert
dun blanc samis mais il ny ot onques
cellui qui peust veoir qui le portoit Si vint
par mi le grant huys du palais.

Et maintenant quil y fut entrez,
fu le palais remplis de si bonne
odeur que si toutes les espices
du monde y feussent entrees et espandues
et il ala tout entour le palais dune part
et dautre et tout ainsi comme il passoit y
denant les tables estoient tout main ten
remplies en droit chun siege de telle viade
comme chun desiroit Et ilz furent seruis
les vngs et les autres. le saint graal sen

ge eue; cont le ne point. Heu; sire seu
li rois escu; uos en noiera deus aucune
part ausi com il afet espee. Lors regardet
uers lanue ostreual et uoit uenir ausi
come abesoing une danoiselle monte
seur un palestroi blac et uenoir uers
au; grn; aleure.

God, angels, and all those things. So the only other thing he knows about are angels, and he goes down on his knees. One knight says, "Get off your knees, you don't kneel to knights."

"Knights? What are knights?"

"Well, we're knights."

"How does one become a knight?"

"Go to Arthur's court."

"Where's Arthur's court?"

"Down the line."

So he goes back to his mother and says, "I want to be a knight." She faints. "Well," she says to herself, "I'll fix him." So she makes him a ridiculous costume of coarse cloth, a kind of a heavy one-piece sack that comes down to about mid-calf, and he looks a simple fool in this outfit, but what a boy he is. He gets on the farm horse, with his javelins in his quiver on his shoulder, and goes jogging off. She trots after him, and when he turns the corner, she drops dead. That's not a good way to begin your life, by killing your mother; but, again, he didn't know he did it.

Just as Parzival arrives at Arthur's court, a knight in flaming red armor comes out carrying a golden chalice. This is a king, one of the greatest kings in the world, who believes that King Arthur has stolen some of his property. So he's challenged King Arthur by riding into his court and going right up to the table where Arthur, with Guinevere at his side, and his knights are sitting, and he's taken the wine glass from Guinevere and thrown the wine in her face and said, "Anyone who wants to avenge this, meet me out in the yard." Just at that time, this lout rides in and thinks, "Oh, I'm going to be the champion." And he rides out to kill the king.

Well, when the king sees this phenomenon on a farm horse and in a fool's rig coming at him, he won't even insult his lance by using it properly. He turns it around the other way and just slugs Parzival off the horse. Parzival and his horse are on the ground. Parzival reaches into his quiver, takes a javelin, and sends it through the knight's visor into his eye and kills him. That's not the proper way to kill a knight, so Arthur's court is now twice shamed.

Arthur, meanwhile, has caught on that something's happening, and he sends a young page out to see what's going on in the yard. The page finds Parzival dragging the Red Knight around, trying to get the armor off, but he doesn't know how to do it. The page helps him get it off, puts it on him, and Parzival gets on the knight's big horse. He knows how to start the horse, but not how to stop it. So Parzival is off on his career.

The horse goes full tilt for the rest of the day, and at evening pulls up at a little rural castle. This is the castle of Gurnemanz, an old knight who has lost three sons in jousting and has a little lonely daughter. So this red knight pulls up. As far as they know, this is *the* Red Knight, the great king. "Oh, come in." They take the armor off, and here's this fool underneath. What a shock. But Gurnemanz knows how to judge male flesh, and he realizes this is some boy. Also, he thinks, this is somebody for my little daughter. So Gurnemanz teaches Parzival the arts of knighthood—how to handle weapons and what the honor system is. One of the requirements of the honor system is that a knight does not ask unnecessary questions. Important. If you want to be a proper knight, you don't ask unnecessary questions.

It's a lovely, lovely, idyllic period in the romance. Finally the old man offers his daughter to Parzival. Now that's good old standard stuff, but as I said earlier, it's the problem of the Waste Land—people living life inauthentically, living not their life but the life that's put on them by the society. Parzival thinks, "I do not marry a woman who is given to me, I earn my wife." That's the beginning of marriage and love united, the first reply to the split between them. There follows a lovely scene where Parzival takes his departure of the old man and rides off.

Parzival lets the reins lie slack on the horse's neck. In this tradition, the horse represents the will in nature, and the rider represents the rational control. Here nature is what's moving us. Compare this tradition with the Christian tradition from the Near East, wherein nature is good and evil but we've got to be good, a tradition that does not say "Yield to nature" but rather "Correct nature." Wolfram is here saying "Yield." And the nature of that horse carries Parzival to a castle.

This is the castle of a young orphan queen who is exactly his age. Her name is Condwiramurs—*conduire amours,* the guide of love. The castle is in distress. He comes in, and when they take the armor off—the first thing always was to take the armor off a knight—he's all covered with rust because this stuff got all rusty inside. They give him a nice bath and something soft to wear. So he is received and bathed and given soft garments and so forth. He is also given a bed in which to sleep the night.

He wakes up in the middle of the night. There's somebody kneeling and weeping at his bedside. It's the little queen. "Oh!" he says, remembering that his mother told him that you don't kneel to anyone but God. "If you want this bed, I can sleep over there." She says, "If you promise not to wrestle with me, I'll get in and tell you my story." Wolfram says she was dressed for war; she was wearing a transparent nightgown. So she gets into the bed, and she says, "Let me tell you how it is. Here's this king. He has sent his knights to take my castle." Good old medieval stuff. "He wants to unite my land with his land and marry me, to confirm the appropriation." She says, "Rather than marry him I would jump from my tower into my moat. You've seen my tower, how high it is, you've seen the moat, how deep it is." "Well," says Parzival, "who's running the army out there?" And she tells him the name of this great knight, and he says, "Well, I'll kill him in the morning." She says, "That's fine." So he goes to sleep.

In the morning, down goes the drawbridge, the Red Knight comes pounding across, and within a few half hours or so, he's got the leader of the invading power on the ground. He rips off his helmet and is about to cut his head off when the knight says, "I yield, I'm your man." Well, he's learned all the lessons. He says, "You go to Arthur's court, tell them Parzival sent you." Well, during the course of the next few months, a number of people arrive in Arthur's court saying "This knight named Parzival sent me," and Arthur says, "Boy, we really lost something there." So the court sets out to find him.

When Parzival comes back, Condwiramurs has put her hair up in the way of a married woman. They're married. This is marriage for love, the mind's love, the love of character, the love of quality, and they go to bed. Well, he doesn't know anything, and she doesn't know much more, and so they just lie there. As Wolfram says, "Not many a lady nowadays would have been satisfied with such a night." And then there was the second night, and there was the third night, and then Parzival thought, "Oh, yes, mother told me." So Wolfram says, "If you'll pardon me for letting you know, they interlaced arms and legs and thought, 'This is what we should have been doing all the time,' and the marriage was consummated." No priest. The answer: marriage is the confirmation of love, and sexual love is the sacramentalization of marriage. That's bringing the two terms together.

This is the first time it's been done, and this is actually the ideal of marriage in our world today—marriage for love. This is the most difficult kind of marriage, because the whole basis of it is relationship, person to person, not to this function, that function, or another.

The point here is that it was not a marriage that began with physical sex; when she put her hair up, they were married. Wolfram tells us that it starts

252

in the spirit and is fulfilled in the flesh.

Well, they have a little boy, and she is pregnant again, and Parzival thinks, "I wonder about Mother." Well, Mother's dead, but he doesn't know it. By now we're two years on. He is one of the great knights. He has achieved fulfillment in the world, and he is ready for the spiritual adventure. No monkish knight, no Galahad, the spirit is the fulfillment of life, not something instead of life. He asks for permission to ride back and see how his mother is, and his queen gives him permission.

So he rides off. Again the reins are slack on the neck of the horse, and that evening he pulls up at a lake. Out in the lake there's a boat, and in it are two men fishing, and one of them has peacock feathers in his bonnet. This is the Grail King, who is, in this story, symbolic of the whole problem of the Waste Land. The Grail King did not earn his position, he inherited it. When he was a beautiful young man, one fine day he rode out of the palace with the war cry *"Amors!"*

That's all right for a nice young man, but it's not the proper intention of the keeper of the Grail, a symbol of the highest spiritual fulfillment. He rode out, you might say, on the level of Cakra 2 instead of Cakra 6. As he was riding out, he came to a forest. Out of the forest came riding a pagan knight

from the Holy Land near the place of the Holy Sepulcher. The two knights placed their lances and rode at each other. The Grail King's lance killed the pagan knight, and the pagan knight's lance castrated the king and broke the tip of the lance remaining in the wound.

What is Wolfram telling us? He is telling us that the spiritual ideal of the Middle Ages, which distinguished supernatural from natural grace, has castrated Europe. The natural grace—the movement of the horse—is not allowed, is not what dictates life. What dictates life is supernatural grace, this notion of some spiritual thing that comes by way of the cardinals of the church telling you what's good and what's bad. Nature has been killed in Europe. The energy of nature—this is Wolfram's lesson, and he says it—has been killed. The death of that pagan knight symbolizes it, and the spiritual impotence of the Grail King is the consequence.

The Grail King, in terrific pain, rode back to the court. When the lance tip was withdrawn from his wound, on it was the word *Grail.* The meaning of this is: the natural tendency of nature is to the spirit, whereas he—the lord of the spirit—had rejected nature. The Waste Land. How is the Waste Land going to be cured? The answer is by the spontaneous act of a noble heart, whose impulse is not of ego but of love —and love in the sense not of sexual love, but of compassion. That's the Grail problem.

Parzival, on the shore, says, "Look, it's getting late, is there someplace around here where a person can spend the night?" The king himself says, "Around the corner you'll see a castle; give a call, they'll let the drawbridge down. If you can get there, and don't get lost—a lot of people get lost here —I'll see you tonight. I'll be your host." It all works out. He arrives at the castle and is received with great expectation.

Now, the interesting thing about enchantment is that the people who are enchanted know how the enchantment is to be lifted, but they can't lift it. The one who is to lift the enchantment does not know how it is to be lifted, but by his spontaneous act he does the thing that has to be done. So these people know that a knight will come and through the proper act lift the enchantment. They think, "Here he is, this beautiful boy."

That evening there is an enormous festival in the great hall—symbolically rendered, beautifully, by Wolfram— and in the course of it, the king is brought in on a litter. He can neither stand nor sit nor lie. T. S. Eliot takes that line right out of Wolfram von Eschenbach and uses it in *The Waste Land:* "Here one can neither sit nor stand nor lie down." And Parzival— here's the key now, this is the crisis of the story—is filled with compassion and is moved to ask, "What ails you, uncle?" But immediately he thinks, "A knight does not ask questions." And so, in the name of his social image, he continues the Waste Land principle of acting according to the way you've been told to act instead of the way of the spontaneity of your noble nature.

The adventure fails. The king is very cordial, polite. Everyone knows what has happened, but Parzival doesn't. The king, as the host, gives his guest a present, a sword. It is a sword which is going to break at a critical moment, just as he broke at a critical moment. He's ushered to his room, put sweetly to bed, and when he gets up in the morning, there isn't a soul in the castle, the place is completely quiet. He looks out the window; there's his horse, with his lance and shield. He doesn't know what's happened. He goes down, gets on the horse, and as he rides across the drawbridge, it is lifted just a little too soon and clips the horse's heels. A voice shouts at him, "Go on, you goose!" That line you'll probably remember from Wagner's *Parsifal*.

Parzival spends the next five years trying to get back to that castle. He rides around not knowing where he is, what he's doing, people cursing him.

Arthur's court, meanwhile, has gone to find this great guy. So one fine morning in early winter, he's riding on his horse looking for the castle. He can't find it. Although it's right where it was and he's right where it was, it's not visible to him. He sees red blood and black feathers on the white snow where a falcon has attacked a goose. It reminds him of Condwiramurs, her red lips, her white skin, her black hair. He's fascinated, in a love trance.

Meanwhile, Arthur's court arrives, with their pavilions and tents. A young page sees in the distance this knight sitting on his horse just gazing at the snow. He rousts the court, and Sir Segramors, an eager young knight, dashes into Arthur's tent, snatches the covers off Arthur and Guinevere— there they are stark naked—and pleads to be the first to ride against the unknown knight. Laughing, they consent, and he rides out against the entranced Parzival, whose horse—this marvelous horse—simply turns so that Parzival's lance sends Segramors flying. So they send Sir Keie, the lout of Arthur's group, who also gets thrown, and ends up with a broken arm and leg. Then they send Sir Gawain, who goes out unarmed. Now Gawain's around thirty-six or so. He's been around. He's known as the lady's knight. He sees Parzival in absorbed arrest and says to himself, "This is a love trance." So he flings his big yellow scarf so that it falls over the sign on the snow. Parzival's trance is broken, they have a courteous conversation, and Gawain invites him to Arthur's court.

So he brings Parzival to Arthur's court. The court welcomes him delightedly, and they set up a picnic. On a flowery field they spread a great big circular cloth of Orient silk, and all sit around it—knight, lady, knight, lady—and await the adventure that must precede their meal. And then, on the horizon, they see a tall, sort of pinkish mule, and riding on the mule is a lady, with a face like a boar and hands that are about as beautiful as those of a monkey, and she has a very fashionable hat from London hanging down in back. This is the Grail messenger. She rides directly to Arthur and says, "You are disgraced forever, receiving into your court this foul monster here." And then she goes to Parzival and says, "Despite the beauty of your face you are more ugly than I." Then she tells what he did and says, "God's curse is on you." Turning to the company, she says, "I have another adventure to suggest. There is a castle with four hundred knights and four hundred ladies that's under enchantment. Who will go on that?"

Several knights take up that adventure, and when Gawain is leaving, he

says to the shamed Parzival, "I commit you to God's graces." Parzival says, "I hate God. I have nothing to do with God. I thought I was serving God. I thought doing as I had been told was the sacred thing to do. And look what he's done to me. I'm through with God." Then Parzival leaves and goes off on his quest.

On his quest he comes to a hermitage, and the hermit says, "Come in and have dinner." When he sits down, the hermit says, "Let's say grace." Parzival says, "I don't say grace. I hate God." The hermit, whose name is Trevrizent, says, "You hate God? Who's crazy here? God returns manyfold what you give to him. Give him love, and you will have his love. Give him hate, and you will have his hate." This is an interesting thought, that the

relation to God is a function of you. Parzival tells him of his adventure and says, "I'm going to go back to that castle." Trevrizent says, "You can't. The adventure must be done spontaneously, the first time; you can't go back to it." Parzival says, "I'm going to do it." He rides off.

Well, the story goes on and on and on and on, and finally Gawain has rescued the four hundred knights and the four hundred ladies and has, meanwhile, fallen in love. Now, this is a guy who has been with one lady after another and, finally, he is taken. He's riding up a hill one day, when he sees this woman seated with her horse nearby, and he is smitten. He gets off his horse and says, "I'm your man." "Oh," she says, "don't be silly. I don't take things like that." He says, "Well, take 'em or not, I'm your man." She says, "I'll give you a hard time." He says, "You'll only be injuring your own property." And she does give him a hard time—it's a wild story—but Gawain's commitment is steadfast.

The high virtue in all of this is loyalty: in love, loyalty; in marriage, loyalty. This is the high, high virtue of this knightly affair. Well, finally, Gawain solves all the problems for this really mad woman, and they're to be married. So Arthur's court and the four hundred men and four hundred women from the castle that Gawain has disenchanted are assembled for his great marriage, when a solitary knight approaches across the plain. Gawain and the stranger ride at each other and unhorse each other and then find who is who and so forth. The interloper, of course, is Parzival, and so an invitation goes out to him: "We're having a wonderful time here at the marriage of Sir Gawain, be with us." Well, as Wolfram says, "There was love and joy in the pavilions."

But when Parzival sees all this going on, he can't stay there because his own heart is loyal to Condwiramurs, and so out of love for her, he leaves the greatest party the Middle Ages has ever seen and goes riding away. As he's riding, out of the dark forest comes a pagan knight riding toward him—it's the repetition of the old story. The two knights ride at each other, unhorse each other, go at each other with swords, and Parzival's sword breaks on the helmet of the pagan knight, who throws his own sword away and says, "I don't fight a man without weapons. Let's sit down." They sit down and take off their helmets. The pagan knight is black and white. He's Feirefiz, Parzival's brother. So they begin talking about their father.

Parzival then says, "Well, there's a great party down the way, perhaps you'd enjoy it." So they go back to the party, and Wolfram says the ladies were particularly enchanted by the grace of Feirefiz, probably because of his interesting complexion.

There then appears on the horizon a tall, pink mule, and on it is the lady with the stylish London hat and the face of a boar, and she rides up to Parzival and says, "Come to the Grail castle. Through your loyalty you have achieved the adventure. And bring your friend." Now this is something. Very few Christians could come to the Grail castle, and here the Grail messenger invites a pagan, a Muslim. What counts is your spiritual stature, not whether you were baptized or whether you were circumcised.

So the two come to the castle where the ceremonial adventure takes place. The Grail Maiden comes in. Now it's interesting to recall that the clergy of that period were such an immoral bunch that Pope Innocent III himself called them a sty of pigs. Saint Augustine had implicitly condoned their immorality back in the fifth century, when he responded to the Donatists' heretical declaration that sacraments administered by immoral clergymen don't work, by saying, "No, the sacrament is incorruptible and it doesn't matter." So the clergy's morality didn't matter, and the result was what they had in the twelve and thirteenth centuries.

The Grail castle, however, is not a church, and the Grail is carried by the Grail Maiden, who is a virgin. She really *is* a virgin. These are people who are what they are said to be, not inauthentic at all. Well, the Grail Maiden is a beautiful girl, and this Muslim has an eye for the girls, and soon people notice that he can't see the Grail, all he can see is the girl. So they begin to murmur and think, Well, he should be baptized. The first time I came to this part of the story I thought, Now, Wolfram, don't, don't, don't let me down. And he didn't.

An old priest comes in with an empty baptismal font made of ruby, and Wolfram says it's an old priest who has converted and baptized many a heathen. The baptismal font is tipped toward the Grail and fills with Grail water. Now, the name of the Grail is *Lapis exilis*, and that's the name of the philosopher's stone. With this Grail water, then, the pagan is being baptized, when he says, "What's this, what's going on here? What are you people doing?" They say, "We're turning you into a Christian." He says, "What does that mean?" They say, "That means you give up your God and you accept our God." He says, "Is your God her God?" They say, "Yes." He says, "I'm a Christian."

So there he is, baptized, and then, not only does he see the Grail, but there appears on the Grail an inscription.

If any member of this community should, by the grace of God, become the ruler of an alien people, let him see to it that they are given their rights.

This is the first time, I think, in the history of civilization that such a thought was expressed. The Magna Carta was 1215 in England, but that was the barons asking for their rights from the king. Here is the idea of the king ruling, not in his name, but in the name of his people. So we have in Wolfram marriage for love, love confirmed through loyalty in marriage, and the king ruling for the people. Big stuff, and in the early thirteenth century.

Then Parzival asks the king, "What ails you?" Immediately, the king is healed, and Parzival himself becomes the Grail King, the guardian of the highest spiritual values—compassion and loyalty. And then his lovely wife arrives, now with two little boys—one of them is Lohengrin—and there's a beautiful scene of reunion.

And finally, Trevrizent—the hermit who had said "You can't do it" when Parzival had said "I am going back to that castle"—says to Parzival, "You, through your tenacity of purpose, have changed God's law." That's big talk. The god within us is the one that gives the laws and can change the laws. And it is within us.

PHOTO CREDITS

tesy, Department of Library Sciences, American Museum of Natural History. **37, 38, 39, 40, 41, 43, 44:** Maud Oakes, editor, with commentary by Joseph Campbell, *Where the Two Came to Their Father: A Navaho War Ceremonial,* given by Jeff King, Bollingen Series I © 1943, © 1971, renewed by Princeton University Press. **45:** Courtesy, Department of Library Sciences, American Museum of Natural History.

Chapter 3: Page 50: Çatal Hüyük, house VI.A.30; James Mellaart, *Çatal Hüyük: A Neolithic Town in Anatolia,* 1967, McGraw-Hill Book Company, New York. **51** (both): Çatal Hüyük, shrine A.II.1; Courtesy, Department of Library Sciences, American Museum of Natural History. **52:** Drawn by Grace Huxtable; James Mellaart, *Çatal Hüyük: A Neolithic Town in Anatolia,* 1967, McGraw-Hill Book Company, New York. **53:** Marija Gimbutas, *Goddesses & Gods of Old Europe, 7,000 to 3,500 B.C.,* 1982, University of California Press. **55:** Scala/Art Resource/Heraklion Museum. **56:** Bildarchiv Foto Marburg/Art Resource. **57:** Scala/Art Resource/Heraklion Museum. **58:** Courtesy of Joseph Campbell. **59:** Preservations Records Office, Columbia University, International NE Studies. **60:** Scala/Art Resource/Bagdad Museum. **61:** The University Museum, University of Pennsylvania. **62:** Scala/Art Resource/Bagdad Museum. **63:** Courtesy of the Trustees of the British Museum. **65:** Iraq Museum, Bagdad. **67:** Giraudon/Art Resource. **69** (both): Courtesy of the Trustees of the British Museum. **70:** Giraudon/Art Resource/Musée du Louvre.

Chapter 4: Page 75: Bildarchiv Foto Marburg/Art Resource. **76:** Egyptian Museum, Cairo. **77** (top): The Brooklyn Museum, Museum Collection Fund. **77** (bottom): Courtesy of Joseph Campbell. **78:** Egyptian Museum, Cairo. **79:** Bildarchiv Foto Marburg/Art Resource. **80:** Editorial Photocolor Archives/Art Resource. **81:** Giraudon/Art Resource. **83:** Courtesy of the Trustees of the British Museum. **85:** Bildarchiv Foto Marburg/Art Resource. **88:** Editorial Photocolor Archives/Art Resource. **89:** Bildarchiv Foto Marburg/Art Resource.

Chapter 5: Page 95: Werner Bischof/Magnum Photos, Inc. **97:** Bernard Pierre Wolff/Magnum Photos, Inc. **99:** Marc Riboud/Magnum Photos, Inc. **100:** Frances Mortimer/Rapho/Photo Researchers, Inc. **103:** NASA.

Chapter 6: page 110: Louis Frédéric/Rapho/Photo Researchers, Inc. **113:** The Metropolitan Museum of Art, Rogers Fund, 1920. **115:** Giraudon/Art Resource. **121:** Editorial Photocolor Archives/Art Resource. **123:** Private collection. **126:** Borromeo/Art Resource.

Chapter 7: Page 135: Private collection. **136:** Private collection. **137:** Private collection. **139:** Private collection. **141:** Private collection. **143** (top): Giraudon/Art Resource/Musée du Louvre. **143** (bottom): Courtesy of Joseph Campbell. **145:** Arthur Avalon, *The Serpent Power, Two Works of Laya-Yoga,* Ganesh & Co., Madras. **147:** Private collection.

Chapter 8: Page 152: Musée Guimet. **153** (top): Courtesy of Ganesh & Co., Madras. **153** (bottom): Borromeo/Art Resource. **155:** Courtesy of Ganesh & Co., Madras. **157:** Victoria and Albert Museum. **158:** Berk-